KEEP
CALM
AND
QUERY
ON

*Notes on Writing
(and Living) with Hope*

Luke Reynolds

Foreword by John Dufresne

DIVERTIR
PUBLISHING
Salem, NH

Keep Calm and Query On
Luke Reynolds

Cover design by Kenneth Tupper

Published by Divertir Publishing LLC
PO Box 232
North Salem, NH 03073
http://www.divertirpublishing.com/

ISBN-13: 978-0-9842930-7-0
ISBN-10: 0-9842930-7-8

Library of Congress Control Number: 2012931959

Printed in the United States of America

Dedication

For John Robinson, who shows me that writing is an act of courage, honesty, and incredible beauty.

And for Jennifer, who moves and breathes like poetry and whose love lives in every sentence or story I ever compose.

Acknowledgments

While a book carries an author's name, it is never created by that name alone. Such is indeed the case with *Keep Calm and Query On*, perhaps even more so because of the interviews kindly granted to me by the fine writers within. Each has shared their time, lessons, convictions, and memories graciously, and I am indebted to them for their generosity.

Dr. Kenneth Tupper and Elizabeth Harvey, at Divertir Publishing, took an immediate interest in this project and worked tirelessly along the way to help shape the final manuscript and mold it into its present form. They work seamlessly together, and their great attention to this project is indeed a rallying cry for small publishers everywhere. I'm so grateful for their passion for books and for the art of making dreams into realities. Thank you. And thanks also to Melissa Ngai, who did fine work assisting Elizabeth with the copy-editing of the manuscript.

My father and mother, Harry and Kathy Reynolds, consistently advocated following dreams. For them, dreams have never been baseless aspirations but instead have arms and legs and gritty reality to them. Never once did they ever say the word *can't* to me, and instead—with whatever wild schemes I crafted—they always responded with *You could do that*. Thanks for instilling that sense of the possible—and for helping me see that "unrealistic" is only a word people use when they feel like giving up themselves. Thanks for your bold encouragement and belief along the many adventures.

I'm grateful to *The Writer* magazine, which originally published an earlier draft of the essay entitled "Pain and the Point of Writing." I'm also grateful to *Hunger Mountain*, which originally published a slightly altered version of the essay entitled, "Keep Calm and Query On."

For my brothers: Christopher, Michael, Bryan, and Matthew. Spanning thirty-six years, we've taught each other a lot. Through conversations, tears, mountain expeditions, or all learning to love a tiny poodle called Cinnamon, life growing up with you guys shows me the worth of joy and the extent of adventure. Thank you.

When my wife and I first heard John Dufresne speak, I had already read his *The Lie That Tells a Truth*, and was deeply inspired by the wisdom, wit, and experience of this powerful teacher and crafter. Over lunch afterwards, and in the ensuing correspondence, John has been a formidable ally and a warm and generous friend. I'm thankful for your superb fiction, your insightful volumes on craft, and your generosity of spirit, which knows no bounds.

When I was a graduate student at Northern Arizona University, a humble and incredibly talented writer showed me how to see sentences like I'd never seen them before. She infused me with a sense of both the painstaking work and patience involved in writing and the incredible joy and possibility in the craft. Over coffee at Macy's and support and fire-starting for what became *Dedicated to the People of Darfur*, Ann Cummins showed me the ropes and I'll never forget the many lessons you taught me. Thanks, Ann, for the articulate, clever, and wise writer and the kind, generous, and warm human being you are.

Many years ago, when I was doing my student teaching in Wenham, Massachusetts, I walked into classroom 106. I saw a man at the front wearing a moustache, speaking with vigor about Ernest Hemingway, gesturing with his arms, smiling and then rising to his feet. Clearly in love. With literature, with life, with possibility. John Robinson: you don't just preach a life of writing and passion and revision and belief: you live it. Every day of your life instructs my own, and I'm supremely grateful for your mentorship of me both as a teacher and a writer. I'm grateful for your love.

For my wife, Jennifer. Just when I think it can't get any better, you go and prove me wrong. It seems that since our wedding day, I've fallen in love with you all over again. And again. And again. You are my pilgrim soul, my heart's laughter, my endlessly encouraging best friend who looks at me—every time I start to doubt—with those fierce, loving eyes that say *keep going, babe. You can do this.* More than anyone in my life, you embody the words of this book's title. You teach me to keep calm. You teach me to carry on. No matter what comes, and no matter how hard it may be. Thanks for this remarkable journey, and for being the woman of both passion and peace that you are. I love you.

Contents

"Keep calm and carry on."
–Slogan of Winston Churchill during WWII

"MAKE THE WORK."
–Motto that hung over Walt Whitman's desk

Foreword

By John Dufresne

Luke Reynolds has given young writers everywhere a priceless gift with his marvelous new book, *Keep Calm and Query On*. Here's a practical, plainspoken, honest, and no-nonsense look at this writing life; a dog's life, for sure, but the only life worth living. With copious examples from his own thoroughly examined life, Luke dispels some common misconceptions about the writing process and teaches us how to sustain ourselves through the inevitable hard times and the unavoidable discouragement we'll face. Write on and query on, my friend! Truth and words are all we have. Write what you want to write; write about what keeps you up at night; write about what you don't understand; write serenely or write in a frenzy; write until your fingers bleed. Writing is hard, we know, and it's harder for the writer than it is for anyone else. So who's up for the challenge?

Luke knows that writing a story or a novel or a poem is very much a plot. You want something—to understand the lives of your characters, let's say, which means resolving the trouble in your central character's life, which means completing the story or novel or poem—and you want it intensely. If you don't finish, your life, you believe, will have been significantly diminished. And so you pursue your goal and battle every obstacle, not the least of which is yourself and your lack of confidence, your obstructionist tendencies, the world calling for your attention, the chaos of the characters' lives, those elusive words, and so on. You sit day after day. You work diligently and relentlessly in joy and in frustration. You trust in the writing process and in yourself. You struggle, and at last you finish your draft. Or, alas, you don't. Plot's resolved.

Ultimately, the way we write is the way we live our lives. *Keep Calm and Query On* is all about process and not about product. Anyone can get lucky and write a damn good story or essay. Writers want to write, not to have written. Writers want to write story after story and live a thousand lives, want to write poems and essays and plays and memoirs and memos and jokes. Anything they can think of. Luke Reynolds shows us how to stretch our creative muscles, how to prepare mentally and physically for the marathon that is the writer's life. And he has had the uncommonly good sense to introduce the beginning writer to some folks who have embarked on the writer's journey and are still trekking. He's included a series of insightful interviews with some of today's finest writers: Jane Smiley, Ann Hood, Charles Baxter, former Poet Laureate Robert Pinsky, George Saunders, and many others.

Welcome, then, to a life of rejection and failure—you're going to love it! And here's why: you get to think about what's of crucial importance in your life every day; you get to bring people and places that did not exist to life. You get to embrace your childhood sense of wonder and awe, and get to put them and your anxiety to good, productive, and creative use. You get to be more honest at the writing desk than you are when you're out in the world. You get to speak truth to power. This writing life is a life of privilege if not of wealth. All you need to bring to the table are tenacity, patience, and passion.

It's a humbling business, the literary business, and this humble and forthcoming gem of a book offers an audacious challenge. Yes, you can, Luke Reynolds tells us and shows us.

Yes, you can dream, but remember that in dreams, as Yeats reminded us, begins responsibility. So accept that responsibility. Sit your butt in the chair and provide your imagination with as many opportunities as you can. And listen to Luke's voice in your ear. He's a nurturing mentor, a kind and generous friend looking over your shoulder, prodding you, encouraging you, letting you know that, yes, it's a lonely job being a writer, but you are not alone. *Keep Calm and Query On* is a book that should be on the shelf of every writer who has ever second-guessed her decision to write or doubted her ability to make a life and not just a living.

Introduction: The Faith of a Writer

I was one of those kids who always loved writing—finding secret places to scribble poems when the house was chaotic with noise, babies crying, my father's farting and burping, the dull roar of television. I had a tree fort in the back yard, and in one corner of it I nailed three small, flat boards to make a tiny desk. I brought up a miniature play chair and sat it in front of that makeshift desk where I could feel pine needles tickle my face as I wrote poems. I was seven.

The thing about writing when you're seven is that you don't care about publishing. Your mind doesn't conjure up images of book covers, how your name will look on them, advance amounts, various imprints of various houses, and any kind of bestseller list. When you're seven, all that seems to matter is the work. The writing. The story. The poem.

Whenever I finished a poem at that tree fort desk, I would read it out loud and, I'll confess, I would tell myself (also aloud) something to the effect of, *Damn! That's pretty awesome! That's like the most awesome poem that has ever been written.* And there was no one to disagree with me. The pines certainly did nothing but applaud as the wind tickled them, tickling me.

And there's a certain kind of delight—joy, really—that accompanies creation in this manner. The ignorance of writing for writing's sake alone kept me coming back to my writer's desk in that corner of the tree fort. Why not come back, after all? I didn't get e-mails up there telling me a certain poem was ill-imagined, or trite, or just plain subpar. I kept coming back to the corner desk because I knew that poems would emerge from my hand and that they would make me smile. I didn't need anyone else to smile for them to be worthwhile. I didn't need recognition, money (Mom supplied all the quarters I could carry for lollipops and candy bars at the local gas station), or critical acclaim. All I needed, in short, was the words.

The words.

§ § §

As a young teacher, fresh out of college and working with high school students at a public school in Connecticut, I still loved poetry. But my writing hopes had grown to entail fiction (short stories and novels) and nonfiction (everything from the personal narrative to academic research on the role of the imagination). The world of publishing had lured my heart, and I had begun the journey towards obsession: *Become published! Get your words into print! Without it, you're nothing!* I still loved words, but behind the love—underneath the love, oozing up like moss at the base of a tree—was the secret hope that I would become a famous bestselling author.

So it came as a shock when one of my early poems received a curt rejection note:

Dear Mr. Reynolds:

I have read your poem.
No thanks.

Sincerely,
William Slaughter

I read the name over and over again. *Slaughter.* Indeed, an apt description for how I felt. But this was only the first in a long, long (long) line of rejections that came (and which still come on an almost daily basis). As all writers know, it was the appetizer for what is a part of every writer's meal: rejection. Constant, consistent rejection.

No writer lives without rejection. As you'll note from the interviews included in the second half of this volume, even the towering greats of our literary world dealt with rejection and still deal with it. Just as banging your finger with a hammer is a part of life for the builder, so rejection goes with the job description of a writer. The first sting is sometimes the hardest — especially when the rejecting editor seems to enjoy finding ways to creatively dismantle your literary aspirations. But more often than not, later rejections are even harder to handle.

One of my most trying periods as a writer was after I had co-edited two anthologies and signed a contract for my first book on teaching. I had started to see doors open, and my heart leaped at the possibilities of sharing words that might be meaningful to others while also helping to put food on the table. So I tried even harder to write more, send out more work, knock on more doors. And then an odd thing happened: expecting to find more success — even if intermittent — I found less. *Everything* I sent out seemed to come back with "No thanks" in some manner of words. Pages and pages rolled off my fingertips, but none of it garnered the nod from the all-powerful editors from whom I sought significance.

And then something broke. The first sting that I felt from Mr. William Slaughter, long ago, came back to trap me entirely with those relentless voices: *You'll never make it. You call yourself a writer? What have you really accomplished? Really?* The kid at the corner desk among pine needles had been forgotten, left to his own musings in a world where the words of seven-year-olds carry power and meaning and weight and faith. But returning to such a world—albeit with a bit more savvy—was exactly what I needed. Perhaps such a return to the words themselves is exactly what you need, too—a return to faith in yourself as a writer, a dreamer, and a creator. But such a faith needs to be forged with wisdom so that it can lug into existence a writer who is not easily deterred from creating or pummeled by the inevitable rejections that accompany you along your writer's journey.

This book includes my own journey—both past and present—with all of its ups and downs, its vulnerabilities, and its strengths. I share openly my own bludgeoning defeats and small triumphs, and in the process, it is my hope that you'll find the words of C.S. Lewis to be accurate: "We read to know we're not alone." In reading through my journey, may you find some footsteps of your own, and know that you are not alone.

Additionally, this volume is designed to lend faith to a writer like yourself who needs a shoulder rub and the dead-locked eyes of another saying, *Go, you can do this. I believe in you.* Because I do. Like most any writer who commits to the journey, I can plaster my walls, and my neighbor's walls, and probably most walls of the homes on our street with rejection letters. But I am still at it, writing every day, because it's what the seven-year-old in me won't let me forget: that words are part of believing in life, that words matter, and that—as Frost tells us most poignantly of all—words are faith in action. Towards this end, the second half of this book includes a host of interviews I have conducted with writers whose works and walks have deeply impacted and inspired me. People like Jane Smiley, Daniel Handler (a.k.a. Lemony Snicket), George Saunders, Lindsey Collen, David Wroblewski, and many others openly share their own adventures as writers. They discuss their worst rejections, their first publications, what keeps them motivated, and why they believe in the power of sitting at a desk and crafting words. By walking in the footsteps of others, may you find your own.

You have a story to tell. Many stories. And should you allow rejection to get the better of you, that story will forever remain untold, unreleased into the world of possibility in which we live. And, for a writer, it's impossible to survive like that. You've been given stories because you need to tell them. Period. If you need to regain lost ground, start by letting the pines hear your words. Then, as you gain confidence and faith, begin again to send your work into the world.

I recall meeting Nobel Prize-winning poet Seamus Heaney for a reading he gave in Oxford, England many years ago. He read his poetry with delight, a wide smile never leaving his face. Watching the wrinkled lines that ran up and down his cheeks, it was impossible not to think, *Here's a guy who loves what he does.* Afterwards, I chatted with him and asked him to write a note to my father, who had written a novel and struggled to find a home for it for many, many years. I asked the great poet to scribble some words that I might bring back home to my dad in an effort to spur on his faith in words — his faith in himself. Mr. Heaney thought for a while, gave me a sharp look, uncapped his pen, and wrote the following: *Keep going.* Then he handed me the paper, looked me in the eye, and said, "That's all that really matters, don't you think?"

And now, years later, I do. Mr. Heaney, of course, was right. That's all that really matters. No amount of success, approval, rejection, fear, loathing, worry, acclaim, or anything else should interfere with the most essential of all exhortations for the writer. May this book be a companion to you along your writer's journey, and may it help to dispel those other travelers who seek to torment you at every turn of the path. May the words within lend boldness and faith to your work and yourself, and may they ultimately help you to heed the essential decision that every writer must make on a daily basis.

Keep going.

Part I

On The Path

Keep Calm and Query On

Now that my wife, Jennifer, and I have been living in York, England for six months, some of the immediate gratifications of moving abroad have worn off. Instead, the steady monotony of life, raising a toddler, and writing have settled in, and I find Winston Churchill's slogan during the war, "Keep Calm and Carry On!" has become a rallying cry of sorts for us here.

As we've been going through intense withdrawal from the car, the job, the microwave, the drying machine—all of which we bid farewell to in our jump across the pond—I have found Churchill's slogan to remind me to keep moving forward.

When my son, then my wife, then myself received the glorious Winter Vomiting Virus (as the National Health Service so articulately and properly named the nasty bug), there were Churchill's words again, rallying me to continue moving forward.

And when our boiler broke in the middle of the frigid winter, leaving our home heatless and forcing us to camp out within our walls for a night, buried beneath various clothing articles and watching our breath rise to the ceiling—yup: Churchill with his pudgy self and wise words was there again. *Keep calm and carry on.*

It strikes me, now, that this is also excellent advice for a writer. If you love the way words sweep, sleep, or creep together, then chances are you've hit your moments of crisis.

Perhaps you've hit that wall where you sit down at your computer, and all your brain can say to your fingers is: *It ain't happening today, man. No way, no how.*

And even though you respond to your brain by saying, *Hey, I promised myself I was going to get at least one page a day, no matter how terribly awful and dreadful the writing is,* your brain simply lays back and falls asleep while the little blinking cursor of Microsoft Word still mocks your efforts in perfect rhythm.

Or maybe you've gotten those glorious 200 pages of a novel, and you've revised it, and you've reworked it, and then you've revised some more, and you've asked a friend who is also a writer to read it, and you've incorporated her revisions into further revisions, and then you look at it and you speak to it as if it were a real, live human: *You exist! YES! You are here, all 200 pages of you!* But then agents and editors aren't, for some strange reason, as thrilled about your 200 pages as you are.

Or perhaps you've crafted two novels and both have been published. Yet you sit down again at the computer, and your brain still won't release the critical voices that would prefer you sit quietly and do something else with your time. *For goodness sakes, clean out your belly button lint already, will you?*

Whatever form your writing foe takes, *keep calm and query on.*

No matter how little you feel like it, no matter how futile it sometimes seems, you must keep writing. You must continue to send out queries. You must continue to make contact, believing that the words you scribe do possess all the possible power and beauty in them to affect one life.

One small life. In one—just one—possibly big way.

Back in the states, when I was in my third year of teaching English at a public school in Connecticut, I gave a novella assignment for my eleventh grade students to complete. Over the course of three months, they would be required to write fifty pages of fiction.

They flipped (and rightly so).

Meanwhile, I relished the chance to challenge them with something of which they thought themselves incapable.

But every one of them rose to the challenge. Week after week, they crafted their pages, brought them into our classroom, and we shared our woes, joys, hopes, and fears about writing with one another. I gave them the challenge because, Lord knows, I needed it myself.

Sometimes, the process of writing can become so mystified and covered in an aura of secretiveness, or placed on the top of some hierarchy, or portrayed as only accessible by the smartest, or the most educated, or the "talented" or the "gifted."

I would have to side with Toni Morrison on this front when the Nobel Prize-winning author powerfully claimed, "If anything I do, in the way of writing novels (or whatever I write) isn't about the village or the community or about you, then it is not about anything."

Some of the best stuff I have ever read wasn't produced in the highest echelons of society or by those who would seek to make a name for themselves for that purpose alone.

Indeed, to this day, the best poem I have ever read was one written by a previous seventh grade student of mine named Mike. He called it "Walking at Night," and it moved me more deeply even than my other favorite poem, "When You Are Old," by the great Yeats himself.

All this is to say that, to write, you only need two things: a heart and a pencil. (Well, maybe a pair of hands and some paper would help. And while we're at it, throw in the brain, a desk, and maybe a room with a view...)

You do not need a degree. Indeed, one of America's greatest authors, Gore Vidal, never even graduated from college.

You do not need permission. Indeed, many of the world's most powerful works were written by people who had teachers that told them they would never do anything of value.

You do not need money. Look at the words of Anne Frank— they burn with the fire of redemption and love, yet her room certainly had no veranda.

You do not even need praise, though if you are a writer you certainly *think* you do. No matter what anyone says about your writing, there is only one person's opinion and voice that truly count: your own.

And should you choose to wade through the waters of fear, worry, criticism, and lack of discipline, you may find that the words you craft do, indeed, end up making a difference in one life.

And that life may be your own.

So yes: *keep calm.* When it seems a hopeless endeavor, and you're onto your fourth novel, and you feel like something isn't clicking... keep calm! Just keep writing. Keep reading. Let yourself continue to believe you need to create and that the words you craft may, indeed, reach the village one day.

And yes: *query on.* When it seems that little you write makes an entry into the world, remind yourself that this is the case for all writers—even the truly remarkable ones. They craft pages and pages and pages that will never see the outside of a desk drawer or a hard drive.

Keep writing, and keep sending your work out into the world, whether to magazines, publishers, agents, or even the trees and the birds (more than a handful of poets have honed their own lines reading them aloud to, yes, the birds and the bees). Query on!

You never know when one word may meet another and start a relationship that just won't quit, and hey, don't you want to be around to watch what happens from there?

Be a River, Not a Swamp

The water in rivers is clean, fresh, vibrant. The water in swamps stagnates: it isn't good for drinking, bathing, or really much of anything except, well, retaining its characteristic swampiness. As a writer, you've got two choices for how you're going to embody your vocation and your discipline: you can either become a river or a swamp. It really is that simple.

Try and recall a moment when you were at your computer writing and the words just poured from you. Try and remember how that felt—the physical sensations and the emotional freedom that were companions of that experience. When we're writing as rivers, there is a sense of writing to give that comes over us. We're not overly concerned about making money or making a name for ourselves, or even about writing well. Our only concern in these kinds of inspirational bursts is, well, *to write*. We become like rivers when we decide that we have words to give to the world and that our deepest longing as writers is to share them—to not hold back. Writing in this manner helps us take part in an experience of gratitude: we become thankful for the stories that flow through us, and readers can one day be thankful for the courage and discipline we've had to commit them to paper. Author Lewis Hyde shares the powerful words of May Sarton, the poet, as she once wrote in her journal:

> There is only one real deprivation, I decided this morning, and that is not to be able to give one's gift to those one loves most... The gift turned inward, unable to be given, becomes a heavy burden, even sometimes a kind of poison. It is as though the flow of life were backed up.[1]

Sarton, in essence, shows us what happens when a writer chooses to become a swamp: things get backed up, and the water becomes "a kind of poison." Who among us would fill a bottle with water from the swamp and drink such liquid, claiming it to be refreshing? We know that it can do no good in our bodies. River water, however, enters us and provides all the refreshment we need.

When we write (and live) as rivers, we're constantly looking for stories and poems to share with the world because we know that our role is to become a sort of conduit. It's not about *us*. It's about the text we create and then give to the world as a gift. In personal correspondence, author Charles Baxter once put it this way to me: "We are here to serve the stories, not the other way around." In other words, our role as writers is to hold out our hands in gratitude for the stories we are given and then to do what they tell us to do—namely, share them with the world. The stories don't kneel before us and offer us money, fame, or recognition; they don't serve us. The more willing we are to accept our roles as conduits, the more joyful we become as people and as writers. The more *thankful* we become, really.

---

1. Quoted in *The Gift* by Lewis Hyde (Vintage, 1999). This volume is a heart-staggering guide to writing and creating from a place of gratitude and in order to give stories that matter to the world. An essential book for every writer.

14

Perhaps no more masterful treatment of this idea has ever been formulated than by Lewis Hyde in his groundbreaking book, *The Gift*. Essentially a treatise for artists on how to live in the world by producing art that becomes a gift, Hyde takes readers through an eye-opening journey through cultures past and present where gift giving is the lifeblood of continuity. Hyde contrasts the model of gift giving with the Western culture's imperative towards capitalism—essentially: make money, and make a heck of a lot of it. But Hyde disproves any thesis that claims making gobs of money and making art are one and the same. Instead, Hyde offers lucid arguments to reveal the heart of art. The more we give of ourselves in the service of crafting stories, poems, essays, novels, *et cetera*, the more we are inspired with *new* ideas for stories, poems, essays, novels, *et cetera*. In other words, as we *use* our gifts as writers to create the most meaningful texts we can, we receive more gifts of ideas ourselves with which to put to paper. The more we share, the more we receive. And as long as we continue to be rivers and not swamps, the flow of life across our foundation of rock and soil never ceases. Hyde characterizes the process like this:

> So long as the gift is not withheld, the creative spirit will remain a stranger to the economics of scarcity. Salmon, forest birds, poetry, symphonies, or kula shells, the gift is not used up in use. To have painted a painting does not empty the vessel out of which the paintings come. On the contrary, it is the talent which is not in use that is lost or atrophies, and to bestow one of our creations is the surest way to invoke the next... Bestowal creates that empty place into which new energy may flow. The alternative is petrification, writer's block. (148).

It may seem ridiculous to claim that our motive for writing changes what happens with our work, but I'll make the claim anyway. After all, as a writer, I am by nature also a ridiculous person—I have to be to spend hours of time each day completely alone and making up people who don't exist and imagining what they might say to one another. I don't trust any writer who claims that seriousness and clear, straightforward logic is what governs his or her work. Because, as writers, we create on faith—we forge characters and problems and hope and despair and love because we first of all *believe* that, by making stories, we can reach the hearts and minds of readers. No logic can prove to us why our pursuit is necessary—we have only to believe that the journey is important and that we must make it. Otherwise, how could we spend so much of our time doing something that holds little promise of worldly success and renown? How could we have the stamina to keep going?

We have the persistence to continue writing in the face of every obstacle *if* we are writing to give gifts to the world, or any small number of people in it. So we write, and we write, and we write, because we know that if we stop the flow gets backed up, the swamp builds, and our minds race with what we can *gain* from writing rather than what we can give *through* writing.

One of my favorite stories of writing as a gift is that of the magnificent Harper Lee. As a young woman working as a secretary, Ms. Lee wanted to write a novel. But she didn't have much time and money to pursue the dream, and so for a while, she did little about it. But a group of her friends — knowing how deeply the desire was inside of Ms. Lee—pulled together and gave her a year's salary so that Ms. Lee could quit her job as a secretary and write her book. That year, Harper Lee wrote a book that has now sold over 35 million copies worldwide and is read by almost every student in America. *To Kill a Mockingbird* was created only because of a gift by a group of people who wanted to help their friend. It was forged because of a gift from Ms. Lee's father, who set for her an example of a good man serving as a lawyer in the Deep South. And today, the book remains a gift to its readers, who see in the story of Atticus Finch and his children a parable for justice—for how truth emerges in the unlikeliest of places when courage refuses to bend to conformity.[2]

A gift.

If you find yourself overwhelmed by the marketplace of the publishing world, by the figures and facts of rejections and sales, and by the onslaught of naysayers who may claim you're idiotic to pursue writing, then perhaps you need the same kind of reminder that I often need: be a river, not a swamp. Focus on the stories that travel your heart and mind, the stories that refuse to leave you alone until you put them down on paper. Be thankful for the gift of these stories, and then make a gift to others by writing them again and again and again, no matter how many times they are rejected. It's in the journey of writing and in sharing your writing with others that motivation comes—never by money, fame, or even logic. Always, *always*, by love.

---

2. Read an articulate and revealing portrait of Harper Lee and her crafting of *To Kill a Mockingbird* at this National Endowment for the Arts URL: http://www.neabigread.org/books/mockingbird/mockingbird04.php

Become a Rejection Artist

The reason most legally sane people don't spend their lives trying to become published authors is fairly simple: they're not terribly interested in a variety of people responding *no* to their greatest desires in a myriad of ways.

Consider some possible psychological notes for a fire-in-the-heart aspiring writer case study. Said writer works tirelessly at a craft which no one else notices. He invents imaginary friends and then invents *more* imaginary friends for the initial crew of imaginary friends to play with. Then, after having all these imaginary friends play nicely for a while, he kills some of them. Or he makes one break his neck. Or his heart. Maybe he makes another become a drug addict or a hypochondriac or an obsessive-compulsive bird watcher who will only eat green (seedless) grapes as he pores over documents from the Kennedy assassination, believing himself to be a reincarnation of Mahatma Gandhi (though born in Ohio). This case study writer drinks copious amounts of black coffee, eats in front of a glowing screen that isn't programmed to a reality show, and only feels like the world is good when he has written his two pages for the day. He checks his e-mail obsessively, and if an agent or an editor even so much as *replies* to his queries, it's enough to make the little hairs surrounding his belly button rise in hopeful anticipation.

In any other job, this kind of human being would be reported immediately to security. He would be escorted out of the building and kindly told to never set foot on the premises again. However, in the world of the writer, said human specimen achieves a sort of nobility the longer he works. The more time he spends talking to people who don't exist and having them hurt and love one another, the more we writers in the wings hold him up as an ideal. In a sense, the harder he works at his craft and his never-ending journey to market and sell his work, the more we admire him. This is because such a writer has moved past the initial early stage of *I Want to Write a Novel but Not Now* and the other early stage of *I've Written a Novel and It Got Rejected a Lot So I am Finished with That Masochistic Endeavor.* The writer the rest of us hopefuls come to admire most deeply has earned the noble title of *Rejection Artist.*

So the real question is: how can we writers become true Rejection Artists? How can we get past those early stages of our work, where being told our writing isn't up to par makes us want to launch our computers out our windows and then follow them outside to smash them with a hammer or a large garden rock? (However, I recall from a trip to Dublin, Ireland, that James Joyce was said to have destroyed seven typewriters by launching them down his stairs when he felt his writing wasn't going well.) How can we get past all the walls that emotionally stable people don't bother to try and surmount? How, essentially, can we keep writing even when the future looks bleak at best and most of our queries come back with the word NO spelled out somehow? I humbly offer the following steps from my own journey for how you, too, might become a Rejection Artist.

1. Before you open any response to your writing—whether an envelope in the mail or an e-mail in your inbox—repeat the following words out loud (no matter who else is around):

"Regardless of what this editor or agent has said, I will continue writing. Regardless of what my husband, wife, cat, dog, children, parakeets, neighbors, and others think of my continuing to write in the face of so much rejection, I will keep writing."

2. After opening the letter or e-mail response and reading it through, nod knowingly. Try to envision yourself as Yoda, Gandhi, Jesus, or Socrates. Then grunt softly, as if what's written in that letter or e-mail is exactly what you knew would be written.

3. Once you've passed through the *knowing* stage, begin laughing. Loudly. Laugh as if someone has just tickled you under your neck, right *there* on the left side, where it really makes you bust a gut.

4. Cry.

5. (If necessary) Cry more.

6. Take a long and deep breath. Grab the side of a chair, coffee table, or a large not-easily-movable object. Take another long, deep breath. Speak to the chair, coffee table, or other object, saying: "You are here. You are tangible. So is my writing. So is my resolve. I will not quit. I will keep going."

7. Open up a new document on your computer or an old one which you've been revising. Write one hundred new words. Just one hundred. You can write more later. Or less. But write one hundred immediately.

8. Give yourself permission to make the name of the editor or agent who has just rejected your work also the name of your most evil, vile, subhuman character in your story or novel. (Note: this step can be repeated as often as is necessary.)

9. Remind yourself that you love writing—the feel of words rolling off your fingertips and asserting themselves in neat rows on your computer screen.

10. Go to the kitchen and get your favorite snack—ice cream, chips, chocolate, carrots and hummus, whatever it might be—and *before you eat it,* send out one more query. Then, after you hit the "send" button on your e-mail or lick the flap of the envelope, take that first delicious bite. You deserve it, after all: you've officially become a Rejection Artist.

One day, after following these ten steps ad infinitum, you *will* get a letter that tells you that your writing is stunning, the market for your audience is perfect, and the editor or agent *really* wants your material (!). When that day comes (or when it comes bigger than it has before) you'll pass into the realm of *Wow Look at Me I Actually Did It.* But that's the subject of another commentary. Until then, give yourself a pat on the back for your current title of Rejection Artist. It takes a heck of a lot to be deemed by society as diagnosable for a variety of psychological disorders and keep on churning out the pages. In fact, doing so is about 99% of the battle on the writer's journey. The last 1% will happen as long as you relentlessly carry forth.

Pain and the Point of Writing

Even thirty seconds of silence felt sublime. But then the coughing would erupt again, sending my two-year-old son, Tyler, into a fit of wheezing, almost vomiting, and crying. Listening to him deal with the nasty flu was like putting my heart through a meat grinder.

And yet.

As a writer, it becomes harder and harder to not see pain as a necessity for creating truth with words—even the kind of truth that deceives (known by its popular genre title as fiction). Perhaps John Gardner, revered author of *Grendel* and *On Becoming a Novelist* among other works of literary fiction and criticism, gives us the ultimate call to action when it comes to pain and creation.

Gardner once wrote that "Art begins with a wound." He should know. When he was only a teen, he accidentally ran over his younger brother with a tractor on their farm, killing him. Gardner's battle with guilt and depression, some claim, lasted his entire life.

But the pain that Gardner so tragically endured also served as a candle from which to draw light for his words. In a sense, John Gardner the writer *had to* tell stories as a way of dealing with the deep and harrowing suffering of his accident.

Are we any different as writers?

I'll be the first to admit that I would like to avoid that unwelcome guest, Pain. When he shows up at my front door,

I have often tried to persuade him that he had the wrong address, or that, if he's sure the address is right, would he like a cup of Joe and a chat rather than performing his duties?

Pain always seems uninterested in my pleas.

But then again, I am a writer. The very best work I have crafted has come as a result of the pain I've felt in my own life, or from seeing the pain in the life of someone for whom I care deeply. Because it is pain that makes the heart break open, and an open heart is a necessity for writing. A writer must be able to then translate pain, his own or another's, into compassion. As soon as compassion begins, so can creation.

Towards the end of my first year as a seventh grade English teacher, I had gotten close to a handful of students who were facing huge foes: one had an abusive mother; one had a dad who walked out on the family earlier that year; another's parents were embittered in an ugly divorce; and the last had been relentlessly bullied.

I offered every kind of support that I knew how to give. I connected my students with the proper counselors in the school, and I got on my knees at home and prayed. But another option presented itself to me: *write.*

I banged out the rough draft of a middle grade novel originally entitled *Atticus & Me.* With my students' faces in my mind and their pain in my heart, I wrote almost in a state of obsession, producing twenty to thirty pages every evening after teaching during the day.

I cried through those pages, and I battled my students' foes—and my own—in those pages.

After two weeks of constant work, I had a quite terrible novel in my hands. But since our school budget was short, and we had no class sets of novels left to read and still two months of the school year awaiting us, I photocopied the manuscript and we read it together. All eighty of my students and I.

Two years and nine drafts later, *Atticus & Me* helped me land an agent, the remarkable Ammi-Joan Paquette of the Erin Murphy Literary Agency. I met Joan at the Rutgers University One-on-One Conference and we corresponded for two months before she offered to represent me (and *Atticus*). The moment was beautiful for me, yes, but it was most profound to think of my four students for whom *Atticus* was even created in the first place.

I now find myself oddly at ease about whether or not Atticus ever makes his way into the "real world" through Random House or Little, Brown and Company, or any other publishing house. Instead, I have found that my fingers—when they write with a compassion that can only be borne of pain—are capable of producing many more words, many more stories.

In using the pain of our own lives and that which we see in others to fuel our writing, we not only teach ourselves to feel compassion, but we also learn to craft stories that house that most authentic of all emotions and actions: love.

And I doubt any of us would daresay that a writer can craft without love. Because while Gardner is right that art begins with a wound, we might add that it ends with a way forward—a crack where hope seeps in.

Follow Your Delight; Trace Your Despair; Fight Your Demons

For a long time, I wrote what I thought editors, publishers, and even readers really wanted to read. (I still slip into that trap from time to time, most especially when our bank account has three digits in its sum total and rent is soon due.) I tried hard to predict which way the market might be shifting, which kinds of books might sell, what types of articles might raise an interested eyebrow at a national magazine. And for some writers, perhaps this works out and they can make a living and look upon the world with a sense of *aahhhh*, knowing that the pieces all fit.

I tried. I can't do it. Each time I attempt to write something because it has a good chance of selling, it never sells. Instead, when I write the things that in some way or another squeeze any number of my organs, then chances are what I write has a much better chance of 1) being more fun for me and 2) selling.

For my second book, *Burned In*, the central component of creation was a question that I couldn't understand or explain. A fact, really: 50% of all public school teachers quit the profession within their first three years of teaching. I was enrolled in a PhD program at Boston College at the time, and the fact was a small part of a massive study which I was reading at the time for a theory class. But that was enough. I couldn't finish the article. Heck, I couldn't even finish the cup of coffee sitting on the table in front of me. Everything stopped in that powerful, sad, weird kind of way when you know you've read or seen or experienced something that is about to tell you, *Fasten your seat belt because we're about to go for a ride.*

And that statistic took me for a ride. I wanted to forge some kind of answer to why so many teachers quit, and the writing of such a book was so crucial for me to complete because I myself had almost quit as a public school teacher after my first year. So I began to build an anthology, inviting other writers whom I respected and admired to help me figure out why such a statistic is accurate. Other writers joined, and three years later, Teachers College Press released the book.

Burned In, as a project, still had its difficult patches, sure. We received our fair share of rejections, and there were moments when I wondered, *Is this thing really going to come together, find a publisher, and see its day out in the world of readers where it can hopefully do some good?* But that project also carried with it this life of its own, this sense of determination that I can only describe as severe bullheadedness. Logic tried to reason with the project saying, *You've been rejected by fifteen publishers. Some of your contributors may not even come through with their essays after all. Why not throw in the towel?* But the project itself smirked in that little-kid-about-to-throw-a-temper-tantrum way and screamed back, *No! No! NO! I'm doing it my way and I'm going to get published and people are going to read and like me! So you shut up, Stupid Logic Butt Head!*

And I have come to see that a project—an anthology, a novel, an article, an essay, a poem, a memoir—that has the stubbornness to refuse quitting is usually one that its writer delights in, despairs because of, or needs to craft in order to fight her own demons. Let's take each reason in turn.

Follow Your Delight

One of the biggest motivators of all, worth its weight in highly caffeinated coffee: *delight*. It's that inexplicable deeper-than-emotion sense you have when you're writing at your computer and a voice kind of takes over. Language just happens rather than is created. There is no thinking, and the words seem to gallop effortlessly across the screen, line after line. I notice that when this sense kicks in for me, I'm often writing for a middle grade audience, my work for eleven- and twelve-year-olds. A voice just rises up inside of me and dares me to try and stop it. And sure enough, onto the screen appear words like *garlic bread, Home Slice, G-Funk, meatball, zany, fart, bequeath, forge, swing dancing, perspicacious,* and *diddy*. These are the words that imbue my try-and-stop-me, writing-in-delight voice. They're there. They happen. I don't create them, but when I look up at the screen an hour later (because I can't type while looking at the screen), it's filled with a whole heaping plate of sentences and I'm not even sure what happened. Granted, much of this will be some serious diarrhea. But during the creation of it—the writing process—delight reigned. It was all about delight. And in rereading this kind of work, delight reigns still. Few other people agree with me on this point, and I find myself and one or two friends can read the writing I create in such swells and actually laugh and enjoy it, but nonetheless, the clay has been made, ready to be sculpted at a later time into something that normal people might actually appreciate.

In the second half of this book, you'll find such a sentiment from some of the writers. Both Jane Smiley and Daniel Handler (a.k.a. Lemony Snicket) claim that they almost "always" feel like writing. They delight in what they do. When they craft words to make stories, they've somehow reached that remarkable place where they allow whatever voice wants to speak its day on the page, and the result is a heck of a lot of beautiful, hilarious, and meaningful work.

A lot of us writers don't follow our delight because of a few reasons:

1. We're staring too hard at web sites telling us what the publishing trends are, reading every agent and editor's blog in the business, trying to find out what they "want." I've come to learn that the real truth is this: no one really knows what they want until they read it. Every editor and agent *thinks* they know what they want, but they're just spitballing, throwing paper airplanes into the universe and seeing where they land. When a project comes across an editor's desk that was forged in delight, and then sculpted with dedication and precision, *that's* what they like.

2. We're scared of what we might write. Say you're a PhD in Macro Economical Theory of Diagnostic Overlay Achievement, and yet you crave to be a creative writer. So you sit down and plan to follow your delight, but when you do, you write stuff like, *The man felt for his nose but found a wrench instead.* And this thought logs itself in your brain: *I can't write stupid stuff like that! I'm a PhD.* So you stop following your delight and you start trying to write serious stuff, or literary fiction, or a business manual. The ironic thing is, if you let yourself write the stuff that wants to get written, you'll find—oddly enough—that it may indeed lead to something deeply serious, a beautiful novel of literary fiction, or—yes—a business manual. But if you *try* to write the way it's supposed to turn out, the project often won't ever get there because the whole time you're writing, you'll be whipping the wildly creative part of

yourself that is desperately trying to give you the clay with which to create in the first place.

3. We're writing for people other than ourselves. As a teacher, I helped my students memorize the rhetorical triangle, the three parts of any text: *author, audience, purpose*. By mastering the triangle, they could learn to craft stellar thesis essays. But if you're writing creative work, constantly thinking about your audience might do more harm than good. I'm not claiming that if you want to write an epic novel, you start by making a list of the ways we discuss poop. However, you might let go a bit of *who* the book is for and instead focus on the story that is pounding against the doors of your heart and mind, asking to be written. Again, you can always revise and rework later, but you can't sculpt if the clay isn't there. Michelangelo once claimed, "I saw the angel in the marble and I carved him out until I set him free." What angel are you seeing? What story is asking you to tell it? If you don't create some clay in the first place, it will be damn hard to help that angel one day emerge.

Trace Your Despair

I think that teen angst-ridden diaries have gotten a bad rap. Many of us mock such words as worthless or as stages that we all go through but really aren't that interesting. Who are we kidding! Angst is remarkably interesting. It's powerful. It's real. Despair is treacherous to live through but a powerful force from which to write if we can catch it, stand upon it, and use it as a stool on which to climb and see better. We find that when we write from our despair rather than, well, despair over our despair, we also heal from it. We get through it. In short, our despair can be fuel for powerful work, and in creating powerful work from our despair, we bid it farewell.

Too often, we writers fall into despair and tell ourselves that we'll wait until it leaves to attempt another project. At one particularly trying point in my life, I had my first (and only, so far at least) panic attack. You've read about it in the first chapter of this book: Our arrival in England started with little savings, no promise of any jobs, and my switch to a role of stay-at-home-dad and writer. I kind of lost it. The ground beneath me took a hike. I fell. I lost all sense of direction and of who the heck I was and was supposed to be for this new stage of life.

But then something magical happened: life got harder. Which was, in fact, the best thing that could have happened. We lost heating in our house in the middle of winter, my son's crib was missing parts, all of my work was rejected in entirety (book proposals, essays, articles, book reviews, *everything*), and the savings got even lower, to the point where I would see newspaper boys delivering papers on their bikes and think, *He has more money in his pocket than we do.* But out of this kind of despair, I wrote. I wrote like a wild man who tries to deny his own defeat. I wrote to stay alive. I wrote to *feel* alive. I wrote so that I could look at a page and say, *It's going to be okay somehow: there are words on that page, words that I wrote, semi-cohesive and comprehensible words; therefore I must not be crazy (yet).* And amidst all of this writing from despair, I learned something: namely, I am a writer. The seeds that were planted in the soil of despair can sprout to yield faith for the future as long as we relentlessly continue planting, no matter how bad we feel. Indeed, sometimes *because* of how bad we feel.

Fight Your Demons

If you're human, then you have demons you must over-come in your life. It's that simple. None of us gets a free pass to pursue a vocation without coming up against old wounds, perennial temptations, unrelenting addictions, and false versions of the people we might be. Our citizenship in the class of humanity guarantees us that we're going to have demons in our closets, and the writer—perhaps more than people in other areas of work—has to consistently face those demons. It's the stuff of good fiction, memoir, and even how-to writing. When a person commits to fighting her demons on the page, demons always lose because they don't have opposable thumbs and cannot bang the keys the way we humans can. Demons can wield a heck of a lot of power in our lives, but they can't usurp your authorship of your own story.

One of the best poems I have ever read—even better than Yeats' "When You Are Old," which I adore—was written by a seventh grade student of mine who had a lot of demons to face, piled up already in his short life thus far. This student's father had walked out on him and his mother; he had suffered abuse; he had perpetrated abuse; he had dabbled in drugs; and he had severe bouts of depression. My student did little work, but when we began a month-long journey through writing our own poetry, he came alive. He wrote the kind of poetry that can only be borne out of facing oneself—the demons that have tried to corner us on our own playing field—and he told his story in each poem he produced. Watching him work was marvelous, and seeing how fighting his personal demons through writing gave his life hope was equally marvelous.

It's not that writing about what causes us pain will some-how magically make our work irresistible to editors or will fill our lives with glee. No. But in honestly dealing with our pain and with our problems, we pull apart cracks in our souls where authentic power is already trying to get out. Every word we type pulls those cracks apart just a bit more. With enough honesty, persistence, and faith, sooner or later we will find a more true view of who we are, of the stories in which we were meant to travel and to share.

Embrace Your Nose Hairs

After teaching in public schools and now parenting my own toddler, I've seen a bit of truth. When you hang around adults all day for a living, chances are you see little of that sublime creature, Truth. Most of us learn civilization, manners, the knack of being proper, and manipulation all around the age of thirteen, I'd say.

We start growing pubic hair, developing organs of increased stature, and learning about corruption, and then we stop telling the truth. All this is a fairly sad state of affairs because even though we get on with one another better on the surface of things, down below where the water freezes, we become a bunch of fish trying to eat each other and then make a show of complementing each other's fins.

As a writer, Truth is all we've got to go on. Take that away from us, and we're belly up. Dead. Done. It's the predominant reason why those who don't live well don't write well. You can't write what you don't know, and there's no way to cover inexperience up. BS artists can make it far in AP English classes in high school, but when their manuscripts come before an editor, and before readers, they find there's a hole in the floor and things just kind of give way.

So when Tyler, my two-year-old, recently looked up my nose as I was mid-battle in an attempt to brush his teeth and remarked, "You have some nose hairs, Daddy?" there was hardly any more room for denial. No way could I pretend that other people didn't also see those protruding black wisps escaping from the safety of my nostrils. Surely, if Tyler could spot them, everyone could spot them.

Backed into a corner, what else could I say? "Yes, I do."

"Yeah." After a long pause, he then continued, "Ready for reading stories before bed?"

"Yeah." And onward we went.

That's the thing about writing: when we find a patch of ground that we'd rather not expose, some of us attempt to cover it up. *I can't write about that—everyone will know that I have OCD and my game is up* or *people are going to think I'm a sex addict if I make this character...* But the thing we think as we write and do not expose is exactly the thing that decides whether our work will be forged by authenticity or feigned emotion. If we *can't* expose some truth, chances are we aren't going to make very good writers. Because becoming the kind of writers we long to be is the same as becoming the kinds of people we long to be: truthful. To quote Churchill for the second time in this volume, "[Writers] stumble over the truth from time to time, but most pick themselves up and run off, as if nothing ever happened." Okay, Churchill said "men," but isn't the message the same for us? We sit in front of our computers hoping to find words that will matter—to us and to a world of one other, or a thousand others (or, if you're *really* lucky, a hundred thousand others.) And every once in a while, our hands find the light switch and we flick it on. For a few moments, the room is bright, and we can see everything—we can grab the verbs off the wall, straighten the modifiers and adjectives, take out the trash. Set the record straight before, somehow, the lights go out.

Or we can shut our eyes because it's too difficult to hear the stuff that our hearts confirm when the words are flowing.

Yeah. I have some nose hairs. I have a lot of nose hairs. I

also have a host of other problems: fears of abandonment, trust issues, a past littered with use of pornography, an anxiety that likes threatening me with visions of terrible things happening to me or my family—whew, and those are just for starters. But if I am unwilling to write about these things in some way or another—by giving such problems to my characters, or exploring them honestly in my own work—I'll be hard pressed to become the kind of writer that matters. To me, that is. Because good writing always has to do with telling the truth, no matter how many lies we enlist to help us in the cause.

Learn to Love Middles

The *idea* of writing a novel rocks. I love the way possibility rages like a rhino hopped up on a trough of coffee at the brainstorming stage of things (not that I've seen such a rhino). I love the way everything feels open, plausible, free. In the conception stage, the vision counts for everything, and everything can be a part of the vision.

Endings are pretty cool, too. They usually make me cry, or laugh, or nod like I have a secret understanding with whatever ending I am reading, or watching, or living. *Yup,* my mind offers, *you totally get this, man! This emotion and wisdom is so stinking deep and profound, but it's crawling into your soul right now, right as you nod and watch, live and breathe, seeing the credits roll, and feeling the sense of completeness arrive.*

But I'll confess that Middles and I don't fare all too well together. I think it's because Middles are far too independent, far too demanding, and much too stubborn for me to get along with.

Middles also take work. A lot of work. Work that involves sweat, both real and metaphorical. This is the kind of work that doesn't gain much recognition, either.

When you're just starting out with something, it's great fun to discuss and visualize your project, so that people can say, *aaahhhhh* and *interesting!* and wonder with admiration about the journey ahead.

When you're finishing something, there's a consensus: *You did it! Holy crap! You finished!* You can use the act of finishing to prove to yourself that you're capable of what everyone else thought you couldn't do. You can stuff your finishing in the face of others who bet on a much stronger, faster, prettier horse with a better built jockey riding atop.

But Middles don't really get much mileage for you. You can't share glowingly with someone, *Hey, I'm in the middle of this novel and it's really hard and I don't know if I'm even going to be able to finish the thing because, well, it's really stinking hard and I'm sweating profusely (both literally and metaphorically), and did I mention that it's really hard?*

Technically, you *could* share the above with someone, but you won't get those admiring looks in return. Instead, you'll get the strange, cross-eyed, *are you nuts?* look in return, which doesn't really help you get through the middle of whatever you're trying to write because then you find that you, too, start asking yourself, *Am I nuts?*

So how do we come to terms with Middles? Okay, sorry, you're right: How do *I* come to terms with Middles? Because the writer in you may be reading this thinking, *Luke really has a problem. I'm fine with Middles. Middles and me dance like we're old friends, cheek-to-cheek, and then we sip champagne and laugh together until an ending comes along, whereby we kiss each other goodnight and think lovely thoughts about our time together.*

However, if you're with me on being a Middles-struggler, then how do *we* come to terms with Middles? Because the bad news is this: they're not going anywhere. In the stories we write and in the stories we live, there are always going to be Middles. Middles are fraught with tons of confusion, questioning, fear, worry, and all-seems-lost-but-it's-not-but-now-all-seems-lost-again-but-it's-not-again-but-now-it-does-seem-lost-yet-agains.

Middles have amazing staying power. Research conducted by education scholar Richard Ingersoll showed that 50% of all public school teachers quit within their first three years. But Middles aren't like that. The stats are even more harrowing for Middles: 100% of Middles remain for their entire life, and sometimes, that's a heck of a lot of years.

Middles never quit.

So if we're going to learn to live well or to write well (and hopefully we'll learn to do both), then we have to learn to love Middles. We may not *fall in love* with Middles, but we've got to learn that old-fashioned, deeply true *love is a verb* kind of love for Middles. We've got to look Middles in the eyes and say, *All right. You and I haven't always gotten along. Like, remember the time I blindfolded you and set you on fire? Or, like, remember when I blended up jalapeño peppers and mixed them in with your pasta sauce? Or when I called you a Squishy Poopie Head? Well, I'm sorry. Really. I'm going to try to love you. I swear. I promise. What? No, that's not me stepping on your face. Really. Oh, you're right, that is my shoe. Let me repeat, then, I'm sorry (for stepping on your face). I didn't mean it. I am going to try really, really hard to love you. I promise. Just have some grace with me, okay?*

We're probably still going to want to do some serious fingernail-digging into the flesh of Middles every now and then, maybe more *now* than later. But if we can somehow keep committing ourselves to love Middles, to find that there is beauty and truth and redemption even before the end, and that there is possibility and freedom long after the beginning, then I think we'll be happier writers and happier people, too.

Don't Be Cormac McCarthy

Nothing against Pulitzer Prize-winning, numerous prestigious grant-winning author Mr. McCarthy. I am just finishing up his mesmerizing and deeply powerful novel, *The Road*, and well, I love it. That he has shared so many powerful stories with the world is a blessing, a *gift*, indeed.

So again, nothing against Mr. McCarthy, but if I had a choice to be him or to be me, I'd choose me. I hope you would, too (choose yourself, I mean; you surely don't want to be me). The thing is this: While Mr. McCarthy has won all kinds of acclaim and, in many respects, has achieved what a lot of us writers think we really want, he is him. Mr. McCarthy is himself. He is his own thinker, his own crafter of ideas and words and worlds, his own writer. And if I (or you) spend my life trying to be like him—or any other writer, for that matter—I will never become the writer that I need to be.

As a microcosm of what I mean, let's take semicolons. I love the semicolon. (I also love dashes, em dashes, commas, parentheses, short paragraphs, and a variety of other hiccups in my writing, as you, by now, have noticed.) Mr. McCarthy hates semicolons. By his own admission, he thinks they're a bunch of little spoiled brats, running around crying like babies and serving little or no purpose whatsoever (my articulation, not his). And for *his* work, I agree with him wholeheartedly. Had Mr. McCarthy used a bunch of semicolons in *The Road*, it would have changed that book in terrible ways. The book, as his other books, is exactly what it needs to be. They are right, true, and powerful as they are, essentially, because they are *his*.

However, if I sit down at my computer and rig up a contraption that slaps my hand every time I punch in a semicolon (or a dash, or any other little punctuation that I have fallen deeply in love with), chances are I'll quit being a writer. Even if I plaster McCarthy's visage above my computer desk, ask myself countless times a day, *What would old Cormac do?* and read and reread his books until I think his voice and style are deeply embedded into my writing psyche, chances are I'm still going to quit writing. Because Cormac McCarthy already exists, along with his precise ideas about what makes for good writing. And if I become a completely yielding pupil of his, I'll verifiably fail myself as a writer. I'll spend my life trying to become him and never find my own voice, my own passion, or my own style as a writer.

This is part of the danger of writing programs and books on writing that stress exact rules, laws, and trends as unbreakable boundaries within which we must all create. Many writers follow such prescribed notions of creation, but they seldom create anything worthwhile, moving, profound, or memorable. Instead, they end up creating writing that looks, talks, and feels like writing that other people have made—to the point where we might pick up a story and not have any sense of anything deeply unique, original, new, risky, or dangerous about it. Because the author has played it safe by following all the guidelines told to her by well-meaning writers and teachers who make a living writing *their* way.

No manner of hard work can change one solitary fact, though: you're not them. You're not Cormac McCarthy. You're not William Faulkner. You're not Toni Morrison or

Ernest Hemingway or John Updike or Uzodinma Iweala or Robert Pinsky. And thank God you're not! These miraculous writers gave profound gifts through their texts because they wrote the words that have been given to *them* to write. They don't follow the dictums of others but work with passion and discipline and create their own as they go. That's what makes them stand out. That's what makes them original.

Consider William Paul Young, author of *The Shack*. Whatever your thoughts may be as to the quality of the prose within the volume, the subject matter, or the literary merit, we can't argue experience. I once had a roommate in college who shared that pearl of wisdom: "You can't argue with someone's experience." We had numerous debates about every issue imaginable, and eventually, he coined that little gem. And I see its truth. We can argue all sides of an issue, but when a person comes forward who has *experienced* an issue in its flesh, we can't convince them they haven't experienced it a certain way. They have. They own the experience. It's theirs, and we can't steal it or change it or disguise it, no matter how conveniently it would fit our beliefs and world views to do so.

William Paul Young wrote his story as a gift for those closest to him as a way of making meaning out of his own experience of personal defeat, regret, and pain. By transforming his own ideas and vision into a book, and sharing it with others, he opened up the possibility for connection and resonance. And indeed, both occurred in a more massive, wide-scale way than anyone could ever have expected. With sales in the millions, *The Shack* has completely shocked the entire publishing apparatus. After all, every publisher to whom the manuscript was sent rejected it out of hand for a variety of reasons. So Young and two others self-published the book. No one expected the outcome. But here's the thing: Young was writing as Young. He was writing out of his own pain, his own vision, and his own voice. A 2008 USA Today article by Cathy Lynn Grossman[3] reveals the journey like this:

> Until *The Shack* sales soared, he was a manufacturer's representative for a technology company by day and did website [*sic*] design work on the side. But he had always been a writer, he says, who gave poems and stories as gifts.
>
> He wrote the book to explain his own harrowing journey through pain and misery to "light, love and transformation" in God to his six children, ages 14 to 27.
>
> Eleven years ago, Young says, he was hanging on by a thread, haunted by his history as a victim of sexual abuse, by his own adulterous affair, by a life of shame and pain, all stuffed deep in his psyche.
>
> *The Shack* was what he called the ugly place inside where everything awful was hidden away. The book is about confronting evil and stripping the darkness away to reveal a loving God within, he says.

Whatever your feelings about the book or about its success, the *experience* of the book and of its author cannot be denied. Young followed only one writer's dictum when he wrote *The Shack*, and that was his very own. This is not to say that the mentorship, advice, counsel, and guidelines of other writers are useless. Not in any way! After all, by walking in the footsteps of others (for a while), we learn how to make our

---

3. URL for this article (well worth reading): http://www.usatoday.com/life/books/news/2008-04-30-shack_N.htm

own. By hearing the personal journeys of other writers, we can forge ahead to create our own.

However, the imperative to become the kind of writer that *you* need to become must be seen as a nonnegotiable. You can't bargain with your own voice, your own vision, your own words. You can change and hone all these based on the example and challenge and encouragement of others, but you can't swap them out for new ones that someone else had already used. You can't become a writer that you're not. In essence, you've got to be the writer that you were born to be. Anything else—even if it leads to success—is failure. We all must write the stories that we *have* to write, in the way that we *have* to write them, as gifts for the world because we know that the world, however few or many people within, needs them.

So don't be Cormac McCarthy. Don't be William Paul Young. Learn from each, yes. Be inspired by the journey of each. But, please, be yourself. Nothing else will do.

Learn to Ride a Bike (Again)

Remember when you were young and you thought you'd never learn to ride that massive two-wheeled bike all on your own? While I recall only bits and pieces of learning to ride a bike myself, I remember very clearly teaching my younger brothers. Soon, my own son will learn. The unmistakable sheer terror of actually doing it on one's own can be paralyzing. Consider: you're high off the ground; you're moving; there is no padding beneath you save hard concrete; other cars and bikes must be negotiated; and you've got to do all this while pushing hard against two pedals so that your bike doesn't simply stop and collapse beneath you.

It takes time, a heck of a lot of patience, and continued, slow, determined effort. Much like anything worthwhile that we humans do in this life: learning to use the toilet, solving difficult equations—everything. And it's actually a good thing that it takes time. It's a great thing, in fact, a blessing. Sara Zarr, author of *Story of a Girl*—which was a National Book Award Finalist—shares openly that the seven years it took her to be published were a remarkable gift.[4] During that time of repeated rejection, she learned to hone her craft and to keep writing amidst the daily defeat. In other words, those seven

---

4. Read a wonderful rendition of a speech Sara Zarr gave on taking time and sticking with it at this insightful blog URL: http://notesfromtheslushpile.blogspot.com/2011/01/nyc-2011-sara-zarr.html

years taught Sara Zarr how to ride a bike like the wind. How to ride and seamlessly swerve in and out of people and other bikes; how to ride with no hands, perhaps, changing gears whenever the situation called for it; how to ride with confidence.

I am not always inclined to become friendly with Patience. I find myself sometimes jumping on the bike and wanting to rip the training wheels off, find the busiest street in town, and ride down the middle of the road. But Patience continually tries to talk sense into me: *Luke, buddy, just take a ride along the side of this quiet road here... keep the training wheels on for a bit... practice turning... then do it all over again tomorrow.* But I like to scoff at Patience, especially when I'm feeling particularly tired of going slow. I find myself saying in reply, *I* know *how to turn! I don't need any more practice! I'm ready for the busy streets and the bright lights! Give me liberty or give me bruised knees and elbows!*

While I hate to admit it (especially to myself), Patience is right. Learning to ride a bike takes time, and the more time I allow myself to practice—consistently, with discipline, and with the belief that one day, I will race through city streets—the more I'll feel like a competent rider and even enjoy what I do.

About a year ago, one of my novels came ridiculously close to being offered a nice contract from a big publishing house. Ridiculously. The kind of close where one might think, *What the hell!?* I had gotten a phone call from my agent who said my novel had been read and thoroughly enjoyed by an editor-at-large for the company, someone who had been hired recently to try and get a few fresh books onto the publisher's list. This editor had previously published her own imprint, and on her old list, she had authors who had won every kind of big prize I could think of. A few days later, I got an e-mail from my agent saying the editor-at-large had passed my novel around to other editors, and they all liked it, too. Then it went to a more formal, in-house meeting at the publisher's. Everyone liked it there, and I received another e-mail from my agent sharing this delightful news. Finally, it had to go through one full-board meeting, where it was to be given the thumbs up and a nice, juicy contract.

Instead, thumbs down. No contract.

To be honest, it took me a while to get over this news. To come so close at such a big publishing house and to have received so many good reports at each step of the way... It felt like someone had been building a brand new bike right in front of my very eyes, smiling at me and saying, *It'll be a blast to ride this, ey?!* But then, at the very last moment, the bike builder found another kid and said, *Enjoy!*

Yup. I was bitter for a while. I went through the phase of *How-Can-This-Be-This-Can't-Be-How-Can-This-Be-This-Can't-Be*. But the phase passed, I started a new novel, and life moved on. Now, a year later, I've written four books of different genres, rewritten the novel which was *almost* contracted for two times, and have felt a burst of new energy, writing determination, and even delight in my work. It's hard to believe that this kind of rebirth would have occurred had my novel not been rejected. There was more I needed to write before that novel saw the light of day, and I can look back at a year ago and actually be thankful.

Seriously.

I know that sounds strange and also a bit twisted. Especially in a book for writers about writing, because hey, aren't we all for getting our words into the world, where they can make a difference to those who read them and, perhaps, help us pay the heating and electricity bills if we're lucky?

Sure. But I'm also beginning to see the blessing of Patience. Yes, Patience, that unrelenting, stubborn entity. Because if

Patience teaches us anything valuable, it's how to ride a bike with speed, precision, focus, and confidence. And sometimes, we've got to practice a heck of a lot before we're ready to journey on the city streets.

Think Small in Order to Think Big

The Great American Novel. A New York Times best-selling memoir. A riveting and world-changing book based on original research. Your book at the front of every major (and minor) bookstore with a massive display. Reviews in every national newspaper. A speaking tour. Oprah.

This is how a lot of writers think: *big*. While we work in solitary confinement, we dream in an unending string of massively oversized beads. And we thread our necklaces and bracelets with such beads until our bodies are covered with colorful jewelry, and the simplicity we once loved about being writers has (somehow) disappeared.

I've got nothing against dreaming, and I've certainly got nothing against hope. Both are beautiful, and both are essential to the life of any writer. Additionally, they're a heck of a lot of fun sometimes. But if we sustain ourselves as writers on such grand visions, chances are we'll never do the small things—often infinitesimally tiny, actually—that bring the highest joy and form the best habits as writers. Simply put, the more we allow our minds to focus on the big stuff alone, the more we'll find our love of writing and our confidence in our work ship-wrecked on the shores of discouragement.

So instead of trying to write your novel and pitch it only to the big literary agents in New York, why not craft your novel and also submit it to small publishers like Two Dollar Radio, Seven Stories Press, and The Permanent Press? If you're powering through your memoir and enjoying the process, why not create a stellar proposal for it and submit it to Chicago Review Press and Divertir Publishing? An agent is an amazing and profound help, but why spend years of your life as a writer knocking at that particular door when your work could possibly reach the world, however small a section of it, through other avenues as well?

So, let's get even smaller. If you've been attempting to write your novel for a while now, but just haven't been able to stick with it, take a different tack. Put away all the books you've been reading with titles like *How to Write Your Bestselling Novel in 43 Minutes Flat!* and *How to Forge Your Full-Length Fiction with Nothing but a Hair-Comb and Floss and Never Break a Sweat! (And Finish It In The Time It Takes to Do a Load of Laundry)*. Take a breath. Get some space from focusing only on the BIG book and try writing shorter pieces. I'm not advising throwing in the towel or giving up on your dream of writing a novel. By all means, hold that dream tightly and commit to writing your book—and books! But sometimes, working in smaller ways can lead to remarkably big accomplishments.

For instance, try a blog. Now proliferating the web, they're free and easy to start on places like www.blogger.com and www.wordpress.com, and they offer a unique way to write for an audience in small, consistent doses. Your blog can take the same focus as the book you'd love to write. Interested in writing a memoir of parenting? Come up with a creative title for your blog and start getting those stories and ideas down. Like to write a novel about a young man with OCD who loves garlic bread? Call your blog *Confessions of an Obsessive-Compulsive* and write it as though you were your character, getting the juiciest story ideas and scenes out on the blog. While helping you to be a consistent, disciplined writer, your blog can be a chance to test material, see how an audience responds, and also to feel as though your work is actually reaching the world rather than waiting forever on an agent's desk.

Here's another option: if you've graduated from high school or college, why not write a piece for your alumni magazine or newsletter? The competition is probably minor, and such an endeavor gives you the opportunity to write for an audience, to get your words into the world, and to feel as though you are living your dream of being a writer. The publication probably won't pay, and it certainly won't cause New York editors and agents to look your way saying, *Hey! Dude! Did you read that piece by Harold Jacobs in Eeensy Weensy Tiny College Alumni Magazine? It was freaking awesome! I'm going to contact that Jacobs guy and offer him a six-figure three-book deal.* No, probably not. But it's still worth it because the essential point isn't to get such a deal—but to keep producing new writing. The more you write, the more opportunities you'll have to grow your confidence, become a stronger writer, learn to love the writing process, and one day see your name on the binding of a book.

Another way to think smaller is to write gifts. Use your skill and passion as a writer to write gifts for people close to you. I remember one significantly difficult period for me as a writer where I was facing loads of rejection and I struggled to get anything new written. I asked a good friend if I could write him old-fashioned letters and mail them—just to keep me writing. He decided to join me in the enterprise, and we began writing missives to one another. It helped me fall in love with words and with the process all over again, and seeing my "work" go out with a stamp to be read by someone I loved was a beautiful experience. It was a small thing—yes, a tiny thing—but consider that I was writing what mattered to me; I was gaining skill as I wrote; my work was being read very closely by a reader who really wanted to hear what I had to share. Isn't that the whole point of why we write? Or, try this: write a poem for a friend, for your spouse, or for your kids. Mail it to your own house so that your wife is supremely shocked to receive a poem from you in the mail at the address where you live anyway. Why not use your gift and your passion and your desire as a writer to fuel the love within your life? Doing so will build your writing material, but it will also grow your confidence. You'll find yourself saying things like, *I can write a lot of different genres; I can produce strong work for a whole variety of audiences.* And, what's more, you'll find that you stop thinking of agents and editors as your only audience. You'll start envisioning people who have jobs *outside* of the publishing world, and writing for these non-publishing-world people is a good thing (since, after all, they'll end up being about 99.9 % of your readers *after* your book is published).

By focusing only on the big projects or the big publishing houses or the big results, we forget about the small acts of discipline and love that make up the life of a writer. We forget about the foundational soil that sustains our work in the first place. Get back to those basic truths. Write for *people*, not for *results*. You'll find that when you do, the big things will indeed come along and tap you on the shoulder at some point along your path, but it won't matter quite as much because, hey, you were already walking that path anyway—not sitting at the intersection waiting for someone to notice you.

On Finishing

inish. To finish. *Finishing*. The more I type and say this word, the more I think of a Finnish man pulling a large trout out of the water, which is an immensely gross and biased interpretation of what Finnish men (or women) actually do. (Please feel free to enlighten me, any Finnish readers.)

But the word is now rumbling around in my brain since I just put the last touches on a manuscript and sent it off to Teachers College Press. *A Call to Creativity: Writing, Reading, and Growing with Students in an Age of Standardization* is a manuscript whose pages are filled with all that my students taught me, and so many of the goofy, silly, meaningful, growing, and (yes) weird experiences we forged through together.

And in finishing (at least until the major revisions come back from the editor), there is a certain feeling of lightness, of hope, of belief that maybe something in the book will connect with other teachers who will then use the material with their own students (who will hopefully connect with something, who will then…). In a stage like this, where a manuscript is *semi-*finished and nothing more can be done until revisions arrive, the room for hope and possibility is large.

It's like arriving at a buffet and looking at the massive table of food while feeling one's tummy groan in gleeful anticipation. Or it's like looking out at a large field *before* you decide to run wildly across it, pretending first to be an ogre, second to be a superhero, and third to be yourself, strangest of all. Or it's like drinking a very tall glass of water and then putting the glass down on the table in front of you and watching the tiny drops that fall back down the sides.

Finishing feels good. Certainly.

But the learning curve I'm on lately admonishes me to not focus too much on finishing. The character arc in which I find myself in this chapter of life has me headed towards this: *Focus on delighting in the present, in the journey of the work, the play, the complexity, the hope, the possibility, rather than the finishing of something.*

And this is especially difficult for me because I absolutely love finishing. I love getting to the end of something and embracing that feeling of satisfaction that arrives. (Cut to scene: Satisfaction and I run towards one another on a beach lit by the setting sun, while a powerful yet not too intense instrumental piece comes on in the background. A lone seagull shoots across the wavering waves of sun-heat. Satisfaction and I embrace.)

But I am seeing more and more that Satisfaction doesn't often linger long. Even though I try to persuade Satisfaction to hang out longer, offering him a cup of coffee, some green seedless grapes, or some yellow construction paper, he always makes some excuse and says he must be on his way.

And then finishing doesn't feel so good. Then, finishing feels more like leaving the buffet, feeling far too full and wondering why you went up for that last plate of green Jell-O. Or it feels like tripping over an unseen mound of dirt hidden by the tall grass of the field through which you were so movie-esquely running. Or it feels like unquenchable thirst even after that tall glass of water.

Once Satisfaction departs, the old longing to finish some-thing *else* arrives: that inexhaustible voice of *What Now?*

So into this realm of finishing-related-emotions-and-thoughts, I am deeply grateful for the interruption of Dallas Willard. Not the writer himself, of course, though that would indeed be fantastically cool to receive a call from a great writer who began our phone conversation by uttering, "Hey, Luke, I just thought of calling you because I wondered if one of my ideas might offer you some food for thought in this character arc of your current journey..."

But Willard spoke nonetheless through his volume, *Revolution of Character*. In an insightful chapter entitled, "Educating Our Emotions," Willard offers the insight that pleasure is fleeting; satisfaction arrives and is connected *only* to specific events, actions, or circumstances. As soon as those circumstances change, said pleasure and satisfaction change, too. (Read: *finishing!*)

However, Willard continues, *joy* is something much more definite, more associated with perception and permanency than with circumstances and situations. Joy is characterized as the choice to see the good. *To see the good.* Love, then, becomes the decision to act for the good of another outside yourself. (Whoa! I'm just trying to get beyond the circumstantial satisfaction of finishing, and here you are bringing up *love*?)

Joy doesn't fluctuate. Its life is more like the trunk of the tree than its leaves. Seasons come and go, but that stable body looks the same no matter how much snow or sun surrounds it.

When I watch my son Tyler, I see something of joy in him. Beyond the momentary and characteristic toddler tantrums, Tyler displays an uncanny ability to *not care* in the least about finishing something.

If Tyler is digging in the soil, he doesn't remark how good it will feel when all of the soil is finally dug up and he can go inside and sit at the kitchen table with a nice, cool drink.

If Tyler is cutting paper (as my wife Jennifer has so expertly taught him to do), he doesn't discuss how wonderful it will be to finally cut all of the paper stocked in our entire home so that he can finally be done cutting paper and instead sit down and kick up his feet.

Finishing means nothing to my toddler. Not a thing. Including such items as *Finish your dinner!* and *Let's finish changing your poopie diaper before you jump on the bed!*

So, as I sit here having sent off my manuscript to the press, I'll conscientiously work to not feel too good about simply finishing it. Instead, I'll be trying to see this state as a step along the journey towards seeing what is good. A step in the journey of joy. And, God willing, this is how I'll respond tonight should Tyler wake up at two a.m. screaming because of a nightmare, or gas pains, or growing pains, or any number of other indecipherable reasons why a toddler wakes at two in the morning.

But I'm not finished with my need to work on redefining *finishing*. Not by a long shot. And hey, maybe that's a good thing after all.

If You Want to Make Good Words, Love People

I might take a lot of heat on this issue. Namely, because the mystique of a chain-smoking, up-till-dawn, tough guy or no-nonsense woman, depressed (suicidal?), dark, foreboding, existential author still holds sway for many people when we say the word "writer." Many of us don't tend to think of happy-go-lucky folks who say hello to their neighbors, talk about innovative ways to get out sauce stains on our kids' overalls, or of generally kind and warm people.

No. Writers are supposed to be moody, lonely, skin-as-tough-as-sandpaper people who (often?) don't have a very positive outlook on life. And this has been the unspoken code among many people—the silent image that we all agree defines a writer. But thank goodness this is changing, and writers are more and more becoming known as warm, kind, gregarious people who can make you feel like you're their grandkid coming into the kitchen for a fresh-out-of-the-oven chocolate chip cookie. While a host of critics and literary types may raise arms against me, I'll report what I notice regardless: the era of the I'm-so-cool-you-can't-even-know-what-I-mean-and-I-think-in-formulas-too-expansive-for-your-small-brain-to-comprehend writer is over.

Done.

Once upon a time, writers could get away with cheating on

their wives or husbands with zillions of people; or writers could pretend like they had some kind of special knowledge of life that afforded them a key to get into an exclusive club where no one else was allowed—and that this exclusive club allowed them to treat other people like they were stupid, ignorant, or meaningless in their existence.

My case, then, is simply this: If you want to make good words, you've got to learn to love people. The time for making your work more sacred than a person is over. Consider the paradox: We write to give the gift of a story, however hopeful or dark, to another human being. We write for a reader. But if we cannot love a person, how can we ever hope for our words to be received as a gift for a reader? We cannot write what we do not know, and the time for faking it has to end.

Writers across the world demonstrate this incredible example of learning to love people while making good with their words. Two of my favorites are Matthew Quick and Alicia Bassett, who started the popular blog Quest for Kindness (http://aliciabessette.com/blog/). On their blog, they search out stories of the various ways that people are impacted by random acts of kindness, and reading their blog for an hour or two can fill even the most doom-oriented writer with a sense of hope for humanity. Quick and Bassett have created beautiful novels, yes, but they also love people.

Or consider author Lindsey Collen, who wrote the feminist novel *The Rape of Sita*. Collen risks her life by writing from where she lives, in Mauritius, where threats have been issued against her. But she continues to write fiction as a way of sharing stories of justice—metaphors for the way in which women are silenced and abused by men the world over. Collen has a great love for *people*, and this love drives her words of fiction.

Perhaps the most staggering and profound example of a writer who makes good words out of his love for people is the prolific and energetic Dave Eggers. As a husband and now father of two, Eggers runs his own nonprofit organization which is charged with tutoring kids all across the nation. 826 Valencia was the first branch, and now 826 organizations are starting up across America, including 826 Boston and 826 New York (check out www.826national.org for more information). He has authored books about the genocide in Darfur, Sudan (*What is the What*, a fictionalized account of Valentino Achak Deng), about injustice after the crisis in New Orleans (*Zeitoun*, a nonfiction account of the man of that name), donates loads of writing, time, and money to an inordinate number of good causes, and still crafts his own powerful and critically-acclaimed short stories and fiction (not to mention starting *The Believer* magazine and editing Houghton-Mifflin's *The Best American Nonrequired Reading* each year). This kind of energy for writing, I believe, comes naturally out of his love for people.

When you're face to face with the very people for whom you want to craft words—and you treat them with love—it becomes easier and easier to write. The distance between creation and impact grows smaller, and the notion that we are somehow allowed license to not care for other human beings as writers disintegrates before our very eyes. Instead, we start to have compassion for others, and this compassion heightens our senses as writers. We make better work; we create more meaning.

I was deeply grateful for the opportunity I had to attend a graduate program in Creative Writing. It allowed me to connect with fascinating people who deeply desired to write and with mentors and professors who loved words. However, there is one particular workshop session that stands out in my mind among all the rest. We were discussing someone's nonfiction essay about a romantic relationship. Members of the class threw out critiques and encouragement, and all was proceeding as usual. Then, one member of the class shared this: "The whole scene feels too fake — too much like *The Notebook* with all its terrible lines and total void of meaningful language."

My breathing caught.

Other members of class chuckled and chimed in with their own opinions of Nicholas Sparks's bestselling novel.

So clichéd!

Trite!

No reader should ever be tricked by such corny language!

The base of all literary work — worthless drivel!

The comments continued for what felt like hours, though I am sure it was a matter of mere minutes. I had been holding my tongue — literally biting it, actually. But then the professor chimed in with her own scorching critique of *The Notebook* and its obvious lack of any literary quality whatsoever.

And then I couldn't take it anymore. I spoke up and said far too much. But here's the thing: My grandfather is now ninety-two years old. My grandmother, a beautiful woman with a soul like fire and a heart like rain, had Alzheimer's and died when she was eighty-six. One of the last memories I have of being with my grandpa and grandma was of them and me and my wife, Jennifer, sitting in our living room watching the film version of *The Notebook*. The disease was already far advanced in my grandma, and the woman she once was had left us. But my grandfather watched the movie, mesmerized. Harold Fenton had worked forty years as a builder — made every house in the span of three neighborhoods in Bloomfield, Connecticut, where he and my grandma raised their family. He worked hard, kept a gruff demeanor, and seldom came across as sensitive.

But at the end of *The Notebook*, when I looked over at Harold Fenton and saw tears running across his cheeks, that was it. I knew, instinctively, that something bold and powerful and true and real had happened, and that the meaning and worth of Nicholas Sparks's story has gone inside an old builder's heart and grabbed hold of it, refusing to let go until something broke loose.

If that's not literary, then I don't want to be a writer. And I *am* a writer.

Now, my classmates and my professor had their right to state their opinions of the literary merit of Sparks, and I don't share this story to say his sentences are as meticulously wrought as Toni Morrison's or William Faulkner's. But here's the thing: the story had love in it. *The Notebook* embodied the essential element of love rather than lust—precisely what Faulkner challenged the young writer to do in his Nobel Prize Acceptance Speech of 1951.

I probably could have shared much of what my classmates wrote—classified as more literary and of a higher caliber than the work of Sparks—and it wouldn't have caused an eyebrow to rise in that tough old man I call Grandpa. But Sparks did something that was inevitably more powerful than any cool-image-classy-prose-writer could do: he loved my grandpa.

I submit that, as writers, we've got to learn how to love people with our words. Because even though we might like to pretend we write for ourselves alone, we don't. You're reminded of that every time you check your sales ranking on Amazon.com, or read a review of your work, or ask someone to read what you've written, or when you take the life you see before you and put it to paper. You write because you want readers to connect with what you've disciplined yourself to do. You write because you believe—deep down in that small place that hasn't been tainted by the cool-pose of the author—that words can do good in the world, however small that good may be.

So give up some of yourself. Stop berating your family

about how much more time you need to work; stop pretending that you can only write if you have six or eight free hours a day to work at will. Love your wife. Love your husband. Love your children. Love your neighbors. Heck, love your enemies (Jesus said it first). And love all these people well.

I promise that, as you do, the urge to create will rise, and you'll become a better writer. (Side effects include: living a better life.)

The Glory of Dirt

D irt gets in our fingernails, and it won't come out. I'm not talking about the kind of dirt that gathers in the corners of our hallways and lightly sits on window ledges, hanging out until someone comes along with some *Pledge* and a disgusting rag or an old pair of Hanes underwear (as was the custom in my house growing up) to whisk such dirt away.

That kind of dirt only *wants* to be dirt.

Really, it's dust. It's like the five-year-old's dressing up as Superman or Cinderella or Super-Cinderella.

No, I'm contemplating actual dirt that is thick and everywhere and underneath the grass. When you hold it, you feel the weight of it and you sometimes have to say, *Wow, that is some serious dirt right there.*

I'm writing about dirt because my son Tyler has a love affair with the stuff (and as writers, we need to, too). For a total of two hours and twenty-five minutes today, I sat in the backyard with my son and dug in the dirt. Some neighbors were kind enough to bequeath us a large pile of dirt left over from their garden, and Tyler and I put it to excellent use.

We dumped it on the path that my wife Jennifer had cleared away yesterday, and then we went to town building Muddy Monsters, towers, large piles and small piles, and also sifting through it to find worms of various sizes. Each time we spotted a worm, Tyler's delighted voice rang out, "I hold that worm on my finger, Daddy?" and my voice rang in response, "Yeah!"

Many worms and ladybugs later (yes, we took some brief breaks from the dirt to explore the grass, and it was certainly amazing to watch how the weight of a ladybug tips a blade of grass back on itself at the median), we went inside for some juice, crackers with hummus, and a nap. Well, Tyler napped, and I tried to organize our little study a bit.

But I couldn't stop thinking about dirt.

I still can't.

And there is indeed plenty of other stuff to think about. There are books to be written, projects to tackle, things to fix, financial situations to worry-over-but-then-pray-and-remind-myself-not-to-worry-over-them-and-keep-working, dishes to be cleaned and generic-brand Lego blocks to be picked up from the living room floor.

But: dirt.

See, the thing about dirt is that you never have to question whether it's there. You get your hands in the soil and you know it right away. It's there. You feel it, and its dirt-ness gets right in through your skin and into some part of you that feels stuff like, well, *dirt*.

In a world where so much is in our minds as writers—where so much is talked about, discussed, and conjectured—I notice, today, how good dirt feels. How real. How tangible. How *here*.

For my current writing project, I have been allowing Robert Frost's definition of poetry to knock me upside the head as many times as I can let it without going blind. Frost wrote this: "My definition of poetry, if I were forced to give one, would be this: words that become deeds."

Words that become deeds.

Dirt is like that. Dirt was once a word. When God said, "Let it be!" and it was, the dirt became deed. It became real and earthy and thick and the way it is today, and the way we are today.

We live in a culture where it's so easy for words *not* to become deeds. We live in a society where we can say and write a whole lot of things but never really back them up or believe them or make good on the promises they hold within their letters.

But how do we live like poems? How do we allow our lives to be so imbued with action that the words we form in peace, silence, and rest are not the Forewords of what we hope to be but the Afterwords of what we already have been becoming? How can we use words that begin as seeds but, by the time their meaning breaks free, become the very fruit that feeds us?

One humble suggestion is to go back.

To the dirt.

To go outside, roll up our sleeves, dig away a patch of grass and then plunge our hands right into the earth, worms and all. Let the dirt get in under our fingernails. (We can wash it off later, before dinner.) Grab a couple handfuls and roll that dirt around like it's as precious as the money we've got in our wallets, the dreams we've got in our hearts, the peace we so deeply fear.

William Faulkner claimed that "the young man or woman writing today has forgotten the problems of the human heart, which alone can make good writing." Instead, Faulkner says, we're writing about lust and glands rather than the conflict that arises out of really trying to love.

One might say our tendency is to ease into grabbing the fruit without ever acknowledging the soil from which it came. We might honor Faulkner and Frost both by trying to remind ourselves of what matters—that before the words, there was the faith. And after the words, the deeds that remain for our progeny are those that were written not with our lust, but with our love—not with our hands scrubbed clean, but with dirt beneath our fingernails.

Writing (And Living) Through

Sometimes, the only thing worse than making a mistake is doing nothing—in writing, yes, and in life. As writers, we often find ourselves stalled at important moments. A character just had an epiphany about how she has allowed herself to be controlled by others. Another character has finally admitted the fear and lies he harbors within. The story's climax is approaching, the action climbs, the mystery mounts.

And we stall.

In life, we also tend to stall right before the biggest moments of opportunity, right before our own stories are about to break open, break free, break the rules, and break barriers. What connects figures like Nelson Mandela, Mother Teresa, Mahatma Gandhi, Atticus Finch, Lisbeth Salander, Mark Twain, Sojourner Truth, King Arthur, and John Prendergast? My list—randomly chosen figures whom I admire for their commitment to justice and truth—is peopled by fictional and real-life heroes and heroines. Each one of them possesses a single characteristic that, I think, is essential to be who we truly are as writers and as human beings.

Each one of these people does not stall.

This does not mean that they haven't faced the same kinds of crises we all face. It does not mean that they have not fallen on their knees or felt their souls crumble in heaps as they cried out, *What's the point?* Indeed, many of them have, and for the real-life figures, it has often been well-documented (as in the case of Mother Teresa revealing in her posthumously published letters and journals, *Come Be My Light,* that she often felt God was absent from her life, even as she chose to continue doing the work He had called her to do).

There is a very big difference between stalling and resting. Or, perhaps a better way to phrase that assertion would be to borrow a line from Mr. Han in the new version of *The Karate Kid:* "Being still and doing nothing are two very different things." As we write or as we live, we need to be still. We should take the time to listen, think, pray, meditate, recollect, prepare, and all of those other things that lend energy to our pursuits. But once we stall, the fight is over. The Chinese have a proverb for it: "He who hesitates is lost."

Living through the confusion, the pain, and the uncertainty does not mean that we deny the fears we feel or the failures we face. Instead, it means that we look these foes in the eyes and speak honestly and authentically, growing those muscles that gather invisibly to push our voices out from our mouths and into the world. The only way to go through something is, in fact, (and rather redundantly) to go *through* it.

As writers, we may need to write through scenes time and time again. We often find the paths our characters need to take by watching them walk down one and then realizing, *Nope, that ain't it.* The same is true in life.

But making a mistake is a far better choice than doing nothing. We learn from our mistakes; our souls grow and our voices learn to speak more boldly. From doing nothing, we learn only how to continue to do more nothing (granted, in more modern ways perhaps).

The journey towards *going through* has certainly been a long one for me—and it continues to get longer when I stop and view the trail ahead each time I take a water break. But when I look back at the path I've already walked, I can smile and see that, at the very least, I don't stall my way through life, or writing, nearly as much as I used to. I still do sometimes, and indeed, old habits die hard.

But when I'm writing a character now, and I find him getting close to the climax of the novel, I push him forward on his dragging feet—sometimes kicking and screaming the whole way. He argues with me, and he often offers an excellent list of reasons for why I should let him stay the heck where he is. But my characters aren't winning those arguments nearly as much as they used to.

And I hope the same is true of my own life.

We Can't Keep Them All
(On Writing as Practice)

One night, as I walked into the University of York to do a night time writing session, I passed by a well-lit soccer field and watched four guys doing intense goalie drills. Two of the guys would kick soccer balls to the two guys opposite them, who would catch the balls, roll them back, do a foot-fire drill, then change locations and do it again.

It looked riveting.

It looked exhausting.

It looked like it probably felt: grueling without recognition or reward. But when game time arrives, those hours spent drilling at night when everyone else was watching TV or eating cheese curls (nothing against cheese curls here; I actually love their delightful cheesiness), these guys were practicing.

Practicing.

In sports, we don't find it odd to think that athletes spend countless hours practicing something that they do in real game situations a relatively small percentage of the time. In music, a similar fraction holds. An orchestra might spend hundreds of hours rehearsing for a single, two-hour long concert. Yet in writing, many of us convince ourselves that we've got to have the perfect words, the perfect lines, the perfects plots all in place or else the idea isn't worth birthing into reality.

The truth is, those athletes and musicians can't keep those countless hours. Those are all preparation. And in writing, neither can we keep all our words. We need to free ourselves to start practicing.

Have you ever sat down and said, "Okay, today I'm going to write *a lot*. And I'm going to write a lot that will never see the inside of a book or a magazine or even a blog. I am simply going to *practice*"? Ever wonder why we don't let ourselves think this way as writers?

I'd venture that it's because somewhere along the way, we learned that writing is supposed to be different. It doesn't play by the same rules as other abilities. We believe this lie: If it's worth writing down, then it should already be perfect. It should be clever, witty, wise, worthwhile, and all without taking too much work. But this kind of thinking gets us into massive amounts of trouble. It makes us think, *Who am I to write? A thousand people can do it better than me!*

Probably. Because you're not letting yourself practice. You're holding that violin in your hands, then jumping onto the stage and visualizing the crowd wince when the notes won't dance the way you want them to. If you can teach yourself that it is okay to practice—that it's okay to write and write without any of it being publishable—then the lines you write when it's game time will be that much more honed, clarified, and strong. The words you craft in the light will hold power and meaning because of the practice you allowed yourself to conduct in the dark.

In the second part of this book, you'll see an interview with the critically acclaimed author George Saunders. While his wit carries the day, something else struck me about the interview with Saunders: he shares the seemingly unfathomable tale of writing a 700-page novel that has never seen the light of day (and which he admits isn't good enough to do so).

Contemplating this fact from Saunders's career, the truth begins to slowly sift through the strainer of an unfounded system of lies that we writers often believe—and the truth is this: even the best of the best of the best writers have to practice. The winner of a MacArthur Fellowship (otherwise known as a "genius grant" which carries the tax-free award of $500,000) has to practice by writing 700 pages that are never published, so what in the world could ever make me think I don't need to practice, too? I am convinced that there is little (if any) measure of inherent talent that writers who "make it" possess. Instead, the dividing line is that some writers are willing to practice, and practice, and practice—giving themselves permission to make mistakes and to write poor lines—and some writers aren't willing to do so. The more we practice—all the while reading great books, honing our craft, connecting with those who can encourage and challenge us—the more we'll see our writing improve, our words grow, and our hearts become ever more determined to, yes, keep calm and query on.

So come on. Open up a new document. Crack open your notebook. Write something without worrying who will see it. Write something for no other reason than to strengthen the muscles in your fingers and the muscle in your heart. In time, you'll live along the lines of practice into the game. But for now, allow yourself to believe that we can't keep all our words. In fact, the only way we imbue them with beauty is, indeed, when we let them go.

Don't Think; Begin!

I f you're anything like me, beginnings can be tough. I am unashamed (okay, I am a little bit ashamed) of my bashfulness when I first knew that I wanted to date Jennifer and, eventually, marry her. I had been visiting her, and at every turn, I planned romantic moments where I could tell her how deeply I cared for her. I took her to a beautiful lunch where we clinked glasses full of Chardonnay. Even though the sun streamed through large windows across her face, urging me with the words, *Come on, buddy, I'm doing my part. Tell her already, won't you?* I had trouble getting the words out.

Then, as we walked beside a pond, skipping stones and watching light reflect on the shimmering water, my old pal the sun spoke again: *All right, man, I'm really working hard here to give you some major opportunities. Tell her, bro!* Yet, I still had trouble getting the words out.

Finally, I was able to blurt out a fairly non-romantic and harried "I like you" — probably making Jen wonder if I was still a kid in middle school rather than a twenty-two-year-old high school teacher.

But I recognize something that I couldn't see before: beginnings are tough. It's hard to really put ourselves out there, say what we feel, what we believe, what we hope for. I sometimes fall into that pattern where I start thinking a whole heap about ways to begin something without beginning it. This is a dangerous zone because thinking is, in fact, a good thing. It's a great thing. We would save ourselves a whole lot of foot-in-mouth moments if we thought a little before we spoke or acted. But there's a lot in life that doesn't follow the notion of thinking for long, long (way too long!) periods of time before we begin.

Writing is like this. When we sit at our computers, staring at that white screen with its tiny cursor flashing repeatedly before our very eyes, then we need do only one thing: begin. We've got to write something, anything, to get us going. As with running, you can't move by standing on the side of the road thinking about how exactly you're going to pace your stride, what sprints you'll make where, and when exactly you'll turn a corner. (Well, you actually *can* do this, but you might look fairly odd dressed in your running clothes, standing outside for an hour, then going back inside without sweating.)

No. We've got to sweat, and with writing, that sometimes means sweating over some fairly awful prose.

I recently began a new novel, and the vision of this book in my head was remarkable. I smiled whenever I thought of the book's premise, giving myself imaginary pats on the back for thinking up such a cool idea.

Then I started writing it. Part of me almost didn't want to write the thing because keeping company with Premise was such fun. After all, Premise was like a non-demanding buddy. Premise even suggested I grab a bag of chips (or crisps, as I've learned they're called here in England) and put on a great film clip while Tyler naps. Premise often told me, *Hey, man, aren't I enough for you as I am? Why you got to go and try and make me, like, 50,000 words long or something? The relationship we've got now is pretty sweet, right? Will I ever be good enough for you?*

Sadly, I had to tell Premise to beat it. It was fun hanging out with him for a while, but I knew I needed to begin.

And so I threw up words and sentences onto my screen and winced as I wrote them. I felt like some very mean-spirited doctor was continually poking me with a Hepatitis A vaccination, hiding the needle quickly when I took a sidelong glance, then poking me again. But I kept writing.

I wrote through my halting, confused chapter one. (Ouch.)

Then I started another halting, albeit-less-confused, chapter two. Ouch again, but not quite as painful.

Finally, I made it to the end of chapter two, where I found one line I had written, and I leaned back in my chair and said out loud, "Thank you, God. Thank you for this line. This one line." Because, see, that was the line.

The line.

I had written many pages, but most will probably be chucked when all is said and done and the novel goes live. But I will keep that line. That one line.

Living, too, is a lot like this. I wonder how often we stop ourselves from doing anything because we're so afraid we're going to get it wrong. We're so afraid that we don't yet have it just quite right, so we counsel ourselves that it's okay — better, even — to wait it out and think some more. The sad part about making little choices like that every day is that it leads to one rather big choice: we never do the thing that makes our hearts beat fast. We have a vision — a dream, a hope, a cool idea — but we don't allow ourselves to begin it and make mistakes along the way. (Like a human being.)

One day, as I was doing my morning devotion on the porcelain potty, I came across the book of Jonah in the Old Testament. I said to myself, *Hmm, I've heard a lot about this Jonah character, but I don't know that I've ever actually read the book in the Bible.* So I read it then and there.

And I was blown away by it. Two things really hit me like something heavy and big (but something that doesn't leave any pain or after-effects). They were two verses, really, that said this: "God changed his mind." Whoa! So God had planned on one course for the Ninevites, but their repentance provoked His mercy, and He changed His mind.

Jonah was pretty bummed about this whole God-changing-His-mind-and-having-mercy thing. But hey, the point is that if even God can change His mind, then why do we pretend we can't? Why do we so often walk through our lives telling ourselves that we must get it exactly right on the first try, every time and all the time? That's a pretty high and impossible standard that, essentially, accomplishes one thing only: it prevents us from beginning something that could be really good, really beautiful, and really important.

As a writer, what projects do you dream of creating? What titles run circles in your head, pleading with you to give them bodies? What poems sit in the waiting room of your soul, waiting to be called into your tiny study?

As a human being, what dreams are bouncing around in your heart right now? Have you dreamed of starting a nonprofit to help reform schools? Have you dreamed of doing the Peace Corps? Have you dreamed of running a mile in six minutes or visiting all fifty states? Have you dreamed of living abroad, telling people that you love them, learning to play the guitar, or writing your own song?

Whatever the dream, *begin it.* Don't think too much about it; just start.

You'll find that when you begin, the pace is plodding, and the voices that seek to nag you back into inertia are loud, but keep going. After a while, I promise your heart will start to beat a little faster, and the excitement that leaps around inside that central organ of yours will slowly but surely crowd out the fear, criticism, and worry.

Begin. Now.

Staying Disciplined as a Writer

U ntil I became a father, I couldn't write every day. I would continually promise myself that I *would* write every day. I promised to wake up early and write before heading off to see my seventh graders. I promised to write every day during the summers. My first year of teaching—a long while ago, in Connecticut—I refused to get a television because I had promised myself that I was going to *write every day*. I lived alone in a small apartment above a garage in the middle of nowhere, and hours collected around me like moths to a flame. I had the time, the desire, and the hope of becoming a writer.

And I didn't write.

So it's somewhat of a mystery why, now that I'm pretty much constantly with my two-year-old son, I have been writing more than I ever have before. Between the diaper-changing, playgroup-attending, voice-over bulldozer/digger/dump truck-creating, there has been time to sit down at my tiny computer and cruise.

Much of what I'm writing probably isn't very good. It may well be that a lot of what I'm writing isn't very good, but nonetheless, I *am* writing. During Tyler's naps—and after releasing my bladder, which is usually quite full—I pop into our little study which is about the size of a single bed, and I write. I guess I can attribute the recent change to two things:

1) If I don't write, what else is there to do in an empty house while your toddler sleeps besides cleaning?

2) Watching a two-year-old experience life in all its surprises, disappointments, and joys wakes up something inside me that longs to experience everything anew again, be it through the characters I create, the worlds I envision, or the way words on the page feel like new beings that didn't exist before a small breath of hope filled them.

Perhaps staying disciplined as a writer isn't that different from being a stay-at-home-parent. As a parent, there's no way to wake up and say, "I don't feel like it today." Even as a public school teacher, I could always take a sick day here or there. As a parent? Nope. No matter how much you don't feel like it, your kid is there, hollering your name at some awful and inhumane hour of the morning, and you're on. Consider:

–If there is a dirty diaper, it needs to be changed.
–Wakey-wakey oatmeal must be made.
–Juice bottles must be bequeathed.
–Noses must be wiped.
–Naps must be taken.
–Baths must be given.

Now pretend that your writing is your child. Consider:

–Sentences must be crafted.
–Words must be cut.
–Paragraphs must be grown.
–Scenes must be developed.
–Ideas must be hatched.
–Titles must be given.
–Books must be created.

Maybe real freedom isn't in thinking that all of this is ever really a choice. Perhaps, instead, real freedom lies in embracing the not-so-glorious steps along the path as a parent or a writer, and one, glorious day watching what you have helped to grow into a beautiful story, a beautiful life.

Cross Some Genres

In the realm of being yourself, I have learned that a lot of writers aren't much different than a lot of middle school students. They find a narrow way to do something, and they do it relentlessly because they think it's cool, or popular, or what is expected of them by their peers (other writers), classmates (readers), teachers (editors), or the even cooler kids in school who have the power to banish a pimply seventh grader to social hell (critics).

Therefore, with all of these pressures firmly in place, a lot of writers decide that literary fiction is the only genre in which they will write. Or fantasy. Or middle grade realistic fiction. Or picture books. But as writers, we've got to stop and ask ourselves: *Is all that interests us in the scope of the fantasy book? Is all that probes our minds and hearts possible in the realm of literary fiction?* I would venture to say no. Just as you cannot live in one genre alone, you cannot write in one genre alone.

I know the arguments against genre-crossing well. People will say it makes a writer lose focus; it make her disorganized; his work won't be seriously regarded if he's dabbling in romance novels when he should be sticking with poetry; her muse will desert her if she starts wasting her energy on projects from various genres; no "real" writer experiments. A "real" writer just "knows" and writes the same thing again and again and again.

But consider the pros of doing a little genre-crossing. We allow our brains and hearts to feel ahead and see what's out there. If you've been working on writing literary fiction for seven years, and you've hit no breaks and you're struggling to keep at it with a frozen head and your motivation waning, why not try a picture book? Collect an armload at your local bookstore or library, read through them, and see what makes them work or not. Then try your hand. Let your mind free. Consider ideas, people, angles, situations. Recall your own childhood (which, as many writers have stated, is a goldmine of possibilities), and remember what set your mind racing. Then, write it.

Alternatively, say you've always focused on picture books. It's what you always knew you would do when you were a kid. Maybe you've even published in the genre and things are looking good. Still, why not try a memoir? Maybe your picture books are telling a story that you need to share in other ways, too. Maybe they're demons and triumphs from your past that need to be written about. Scribing your own memoir will allow an entirely unprecedented level of creativity to burst forth from your fingers in trembling excitement.

When I was a teacher, I was always amazed when I met other teachers of different grade levels. If I was teaching high school seniors and I talked with someone who taught only freshmen, she might say, "Ugh, I don't know how you do it. I could never teach seniors." But then, when I switched to teach freshmen, someone else would say, "Ugh, I don't know how you do it. I could never teach freshmen. I love my seniors." For a long time, I thought that it was as simple as it sounded: some teachers were strictly able to teach certain students. But the more I worked with other teachers and continued my own journey in the classroom, the more I began to see that it's a mind block rather than any real inability that makes teachers say such things, because they could. Most teachers could switch grades and teach different levels if they really wanted to and if they were willing to fail during the process of learning how to do it effectively. The real preventative measure, however, is the age-old human yearning for comfort. We say, *Once I've found any kind of ability or success, then I'm staying right where I am. I don't need to try anything else. Why should I?*

When it comes to writing, whether you've experienced publication or not, trying to write in different genres is crucial to your ability to be creative, to stay passionate about your craft, and to resist what so many other people want you to believe about writing. The truth is much more simple and much more liberating: if you love to write, then you love to write. You allow yourself the flexibility to try different forms, styles, and yes, genres. In doing so, you may discover hidden gems you never knew were waiting at the tips of your fingers, itching to crawl out and dive onto the pages if you would only give them a shot.

Make Yourself a Tea Box

One of the best gifts I have ever received from anyone was a tea box that Jennifer gave me one month before I turned thirty. That night, she called our son, Tyler, into the hallway just outside our living room, whispered something into his ear, and then sent him rushing and smiling towards me.

When Tyler said, "Here you go, Daddy," and then handed me a Twinings tea box, I thought, *Hey, tea, not so bad. I guess I can make a hot cup of tea and that will help me take a breath, relax, maybe drink it while I pick up the novel tonight after Tyler goes to bed...* But then Jennifer followed after Tyler saying, "Well, it's thirty days until you turn thirty, so I wanted to start the countdown. Open it up and check it out."

Her smile grew wider as she watched me, and then I knew: *This is going to be a heck of a lot better than Twinings Tea.* Nothing against you, if you're reading this and you happen to love Twinings Tea or work for Twinings Tea. Or had a dream last night that you had actually transmogrified into a Twinings tea bag and are now struggling with the weight of disappointment as you are slowly—*slowly*—coming to terms with the fact that you are not, in fact, a Twinings tea bag, but instead are a human being.

And it was. It was a *heck* of a lot better than Twinings Tea.

Inside this gem of a box were thirty index cards, all folded up, on which thirty sayings about writing had been lovingly scribed by Jennifer's hand. I began pulling out the inspiring little quotes and was delighted to read the wisdom, advice, challenge, and encouragement of so many remarkable writers. To say the least, it gave me the slight edge over a writer's constant companion: the gravity that seems to push his hand away from the letters of a keyboard.

Like a little kid, I read through each quote immediately until I had stuffed the wisdom of all thirty into my brain. Then I read them all again. Now, I keep that little tea box in my study on a small shelf right above my writing desk. Before I begin a writing session, I randomly pull out a quote and read it, allowing its meaning to send some juice to my tired or begrudging fingers. If I get a particularly bad rejection, I can go to my tea box and read a line (or two, or three, or even all thirty again, depending on how bad the rejection is). I find that I'm memorizing these little sayings, and as the sayings become permanent signposts along the roadways of my brain, I find I'm also living them out more and more.

Make yourself a tea box. Collect the quotes and sayings on writing that move and motivate you. As you read books, blogs, and connect with other writers, catch the lines that tug at your writer's nerve and record them for your tea box. Keep it close by. To get you started, here are a few of my favorites that have made their way into my tea box:

"I write when I am inspired, and I see to it that I'm inspired at nine o'clock every morning." —Peter DeVries

"There's nothing to writing. All you do is sit down at a typewriter and open a vein." —Walter Wellesley "Red" Smith

"I hear and I forget, I see and I remember, I write and I understand." —Chinese Proverb

"One of the marks of a gift is to have the courage to use it."
—Katherine Anne Porter

"Suit the action to the word, the word to the action." —William
Shakespeare

*"Keep away from people who try to belittle your ambitions. Small
people always do that, but the really great make you feel that you,
too, can become great."* —Mark Twain

*"The difference between the right word and the almost right word is
the difference between lightning and the lightning bug."* —Mark
Twain

*"Every author in some way portrays himself in his works, even if it
is against his will."* —Goethe

"I'm going to write because I cannot help it." —Charlotte Bronte

*"Close the door. Write with no one looking over your shoulder.
Don't try to figure out what other people want to hear from you;
figure out what you have to say. It's the one and only thing you
have to offer."* —Barbara Kingsolver

*"No, it's not a very good story—its author was too busy listening
to other voices to listen as closely as he should have to the one coming
from inside."* —Stephen King

*"Find out the reason that commands you to write; see whether it
has spread its roots into the very depth of your heart; confess to
yourself you would have to die if you were forbidden to write."*
—Rainer Maria Rilke

"To live a creative life, we must lose our fear of being wrong."
—Claude M. Bristol

"Writing a novel is like driving a car at night. You can see only as far as your headlights, but you can make the whole trip that way."
—E.L. Doctorow

"No tears in the writer, no tears in the reader. No surprise in the writer, no surprise in the reader." —Robert Frost

"Work is love made visible. And if you cannot work with love but only distaste, it is better that you should leave your work and sit at the gate of a temple and take alms of those who work with joy."
—Kahlil Gibran

"Any work of art must first of all tell a story." —Robert Frost

"Only write from your own passion, your own truth. That's the only thing you really know about, and anything else leads you away from the pulse." —Marianne Williamson

It's Not about Results

When I was a middle school teacher, I always told my students that it wasn't about the grades. It wasn't about any score or any comparison, it wasn't about making the team, and it wasn't about winning something. Instead, it is always, *always* about the work you put into it and the way you keep facing the challenges that show up on your doorstep. That's it.

I was pretty good at giving the above message in bold ways. Using stories and examples, I could make it funny. I could make it poignant. I could make it look and feel and walk and talk like truth. But I didn't realize until a few nights ago how I still needed to learn to believe it myself, and it's thanks to my wife and her breaking through a core belief I hadn't changed.

It had been one of those long days where the sky hangs heavy, telling you, *Hey, man, don't even try to come out, because as soon as you do, I am going to* pour *on you. I'm not just talking drizzle; I am talking about sheets of water cascading across your face so fast and hard you'll think you're on the inside of a high-powered washing machine, heavy-duty cycle.* So we made the best of indoor time, doing puzzles, pretending to be joint Bobs the Builder, running back and forth between the washing machine in our kitchen and the front door, banging on buckets, making trucks talk, and trading tickles. By the end of the day, I was wiped. Exhausted.

When I'm tired, my mind usually races with failures—things I have worked really hard at but which haven't come to fruition. It's like being overtired triggers something inside me that says, *Ah, but Luke! If you could only work a little harder, you would have had success in this area!*

This particular night, it happened to be the voice of condemnation over my writing.

My writing had come pretty darn close to being published a couple of times, and every time, I would hold my head up high and say, *Getting there… getting there,* and keep trying. Meanwhile, I kept telling myself what I had heard hundreds of writers say you must do as you wait for a book to make the rounds with editors: *keep writing.* So, what did I do?

I kept writing. I wrote ferociously. I wrote every story that popped into my head, which was a lot, I found, when you have an overactive imagination and some solid writing time at your disposal while your son is napping. But when the passes continued to come, I started to feel like I did when I was in high school, playing basketball. Well, perhaps it's a misnomer to say *playing* basketball.

The truth is I didn't do much playing during the games. I made my high school basketball team, which was a steep challenge. We had a big school, there were a lot of strong players, and our team won the state championship a couple of times. I made the team and worked hard under our demanding but wise coach, whose day job was being a prison guard. In the off seasons, I worked four or five hours a day practicing drills, running miles dribbling two basketballs, sprinting suicides, shooting hundreds of free throws, and completing shooting drills that included sit-ups and push-ups mixed in between shots.

In short, I worked my butt off, ate zero bad food, and turned the spotlights on above our garage to do night drills when it grew too dark to see. But no matter how hard I worked, I didn't ever play much in the games. It was like there was this mental block, making me afraid on the court, causing me to hesitate, to doubt I could make the same shots that I made thousands of times in my own driveway every day. Throughout my entire high school basketball-playing journey, I probably played less than the thirty-two minutes of a full game.

Afterwards, I looked back at that experience and dealt with what happened by telling myself things like, *Well, I learned a lot from it* and, *I worked really hard, and I became very physically fit and healthy, right?* And I kind of thought that it was over and done with. Old news. Moved on. But it was only in talking with Jennifer a few nights ago, as I began to bemoan my lack of getting a contract for *Atticus & Me*, that she asked me about my high school basketball experience. Even though it was years ago, the first thing that popped out of my mouth was, "It was an utter failure."

Jen: An *utter failure?!* Do you really think that?

Me: Well, I know I learned a lot and all that… but, really, my goal was to play, and I never accomplished that. So, yeah, it was a failure, essentially."

Jen gives me this knowing look—but kind of sprinkled with confusion and doesn't say anything. But her not-saying-anything look says the following to me in very clear words: *Whoa, buddy, you are way off here, and I'm going to give you a minute to really let how off you are sink in… think about what you just said… and think about what is really true, deep down.*

Me: Wasn't it? A failure, I mean…

Jen: NOT AT ALL!

Me: Why not?

Jen: Because you worked at it. Every day you were out there busting your butt when most other high school kids wouldn't have been able to do half of what you did—the way you worked, the discipline you learned. It was never about making shots in the game. It was always about the person you were learning to become.

Me: (Okay, I'll be honest: tears.)

Jen: Achievements are like tiny dots on a long line. The line is the journey you take—the way you work at something, the way you live—and achievements and results are just single points. Do you really think that your life is all about the dots and not the lines?

Me: Well, when you put it that way…

Jen's look says, *Now, you're finally starting to get it.*

And the truth is, I am. Starting to get it, I mean. It's what I always told my students and what I *really* wanted them to believe and make a part of their lives in the deep kind of way that core beliefs become a part of all of our lives. But even though I knew what to say to my students, I hadn't yet destroyed my own false belief. I wasn't a failure because I didn't play much basketball in high school. And as a writer, I'm not a failure because *Atticus & Me* hasn't yet garnered a publishing contract.

Instead, I'm finally learning to live out what I've often preached thanks to my wife, who challenged me to face the lies I'd been telling myself. I'm finally learning that it isn't about those tiny dots on the long lines of our lives that count. It isn't about the results.

It's about something much more beautiful. It's about the way we draw those lines, the directions we send them towards, and the way they intersect other lines along the path they take.

Be Defiant

The word *defiance* seems like it should be the name of a cologne, or a perfume, or a mixture of both. Defiance: the new smell for men and women who like to live defying everything, and for men and women who like to live defying defiance, even. From Calvin Klein, and from Other Famous People who Create Smells that are Encapsulated with One-Word Nouns with Super-Strong Ties to Verbs.

Defiance, I'm learning, is instead the name of the game when raising a toddler. Tyler is now two and a half years old, and Defiance has emerged in all its glorious, confusing, hair-raising, skin-tingling, tear-producing manifestations.

And, I will confess, I wasn't ready for it. However, my toddler's dance with Defiance is teaching me more than any graduate writing program ever could, more than any mentor, even. More than any book, any course, any workshop, any seminar, any software, any publication—in short, more than anything. Seeing Defiance play out in my toddler's life shows me the exact characteristic that every writer needs in order to make it for the long haul of this surprising journey.

When Defiance first showed up in my son, I was still patting myself on the back a bit for a semi-smooth switch to stay-at-home parenting and writing instead of making my way into the public school each day to work with my lovely seventh graders. I deeply missed teaching, but I was ecstatic to have such intense time with our son. To watch him laugh, smile, dig, point out construction vehicles, point out colors, people, people's hair, and people's various, multi-colored shoes.

Enter Defiance.

Where our days once progressed with ease and the occasional refusal to comply, they now progress with multiple battles proceeding the ever more embittered struggles for power. Where once the marvelous technique of distraction could be employed to swiftly overcome most any problem—*Oh, you wanted to wear a diaper on your head? Hey, look at that dog walking down the sidewalk; let's go see it!*—now Distraction has been bypassed for Defiance.

Then: *Oh, you want to eat lollipops for dinner? Hey, check out all this ketchup we can put on your veggie nuggets! Whoa, Dude! Ketchup everywhere! Quick, eat the Veggie Nuggets before they drown in ketchup!* Problem solved.

Now: *Oh, you want to wear the same Thomas the Tank Engine shirt that you've been wearing for two days straight and which is now covered in a mixture of dirt, various sauces, mucus, and pesto? Hey, check out this* super *cool Bob the Builder shirt you can wear instead! No? Really, no? You sure you don't want to wear this* Bob the Builder shirt *while I pick you up and swing you around while I sing the theme song for* Bob the Builder *and then jump up and down pretending to be a kangaroo who's looking for lollipops in the* magical forest?

No?

Really?

Did you hear all the things I said?

And so, Defiance has entered the game. It was a late substitution, as I honestly thought we were going to skate through the toddler stage with our greatest difficulty being a few broken bananas here and there that we could not glue together (a perennial and incomprehensible frustration of Tyler's).

But then, the buzzer sounded and the opposing team put in the sub from the end of the bench. He's a little guy, but the thing is, he's that kind of player who will dive for loose balls, smash his head into the bleachers to keep the basketball in bounds, and toss up a shot from half-court to send the game into overtime (and swish it).

Defiance is a scrappy player, and he lets nothing pass no matter how small.

You want to take a bath?

No.

You want to take a shower?

No.

You want to take a bath and shower at the same time? So cool! *Right?*

No.

All the parenting books I've been reading (and there are a lot of them out there) tell me this is completely normal. They say that every toddler has to pass through this stage where they want independence but they don't really want it, no, yes they do want it, no, actually, they don't. No, yes, they do. I mean, they don't.

The books assure me that this stage will pass and that the important thing is to remain calm, to be firm but loving, and to try not to make a big deal over small things and let go of the battles that really aren't that important. The books tell me that not fighting your toddler over every little thing will help the stage pass more quickly, and things will again begin to resemble that peaceful euphoria for which I had been on my knees praising God.

And I trust that Defiance, as it faces my slow, calm, determined will to wear it down, will eventually give up a bit of its power and a form of Compliance will eventually take its place.

But here's where the writer can't be like the toddler. Every writer has at least a modicum of the toddler's talent for Defiance inside of her. She has to, or else why would she keep sending her work out to magazines and editors after being told *No* relentlessly? Defiance. She has it. She believes that she knows better than each editor who has rejected every single one of her stories, poems, books, or articles.

The toddler's companionship with Defiance is not based on logic. The toddler just has an irrepressible amount of stamina and determination to focus on the *one thing* he wants, and he will refuse any kind of substitution, compromise, or giving up of that drive. The writer's companionship with Defiance takes the same tack. Where the toddler and the writer differ, however, is in possession of the frontal lobes.

See, the toddler doesn't yet have fully developed frontal lobes in his brain, which, in layman's terms, means that the toddler is so friendly with Defiance because he doesn't yet have the ability to reason effectively, to use logic to enhance his thinking so that he can come to rational, sane conclusions. The frontal lobes are the logic lobes—the source of clear, sense-making thinking, you might say. So, once these frontal lobes kick in for the toddler—along with some consistent, loving parenting—the show time for Defiance starts to wind down.

Meanwhile, the writer already *has* these frontal lobes— supposedly fully developed. But where the toddler learns to use his effectively, the writer must somehow learn to silence hers. Karl Marx called logic "the money of the mind." In this regard, Marx was right: we use logic to help us classify why we make certain decisions, what is worth our time and energy, and essentially, how it all will end when tallied with dollar signs.

The writer's allegiance lies along a higher plane. Higher than logic. Higher than money. The writer must learn to live above what makes sense. After all, who can come up with a logical defense for sitting alone in a room for hours each day typing words then erasing them, typing words then erasing them again, staying up late into the night or waking up early to do it, receiving little or often no pay, and yet keeping at it day after day after day? Even the best trial lawyer in the country would be hard-pressed to defend such an activity.

But the reason we write isn't to make money. Deep down, we know this. And the reason we write isn't to achieve fame. Deep down, we know this, too. The reason we write isn't even to prove something.

At the core, the reason we write is because we have to. Because we love the process and the journey and the act of creating stories so much that were it taken away from us, it would be as evil as depriving a toddler of the ability to laugh.

We write for the same reason a toddler befriends Defiance: it's what we have to do. There's no way around the stage for a toddler, and if you're a writer, there's no way to shake the stories out of your soul except by committing them to paper. And once we do that, new ones always show up to plead their right to be born.

So be defiant. Write not because of reason or because of logic. Write because it's who you are, a part of you just as deep and meaningful as your eyes, your hope, your truth. Write because of love. And write with fire.

Part II

Finding Footsteps

In the following section of the book, fourteen authors share their wisdom, wit, insight, and experiences as writers who care deeply about craft, process, and the power of words. Each author openly shares experiences of rejection, publication, and the road to and from both.

My hope is that their words serve as footsteps for your own journey. May the following stories continue to help you see that you are not—indeed, never have been and never will be—alone. And may they lend you courage to carry on.

George Saunders

As a young man, George Saunders didn't initially pursue a career in creative writing, which is surprising considering all that he has already accomplished in the literary world. He attended college at the Colorado School of Mines, in Golden, Colorado, where he earned a B.S. in Geophysical Engineering. For many years following his graduation, he worked as a technical writer and geophysical engineer. He only applied to Syracuse University's Creative Writing MA program after he read about it in *People* magazine.

Saunders' list of critically acclaimed work includes the short story collections *CivilWarLand in Bad Decline* (Random House, 1996), *Pastoralia* (Riverhead, 2000), *In Persuasion Nation* (Riverhead, 2006), and the collection of essays, *The Braindead Megaphone* (Riverhead, 2007). Saunders has been a recipient of the MacArthur Grant, also known as the "genius grant," and is currently a Professor in the Creative Writing program at Syracuse University.

How does your background and undergraduate study in geophysical engineering influence your writing?

Well, it infused me with a sense of cruel, irrational rigor. In engineering school, it was made clear to us that effort didn't matter, only results. So you could work and work, and if you came up with the wrong answer, too bad. No partial credit.

This comes in handy during the rewriting phase (!). This background also got me into some odd and restricted places. My first job was on a field seismic crew in Sumatra, Indonesia. We did field seismic work in virgin jungles, forests that very few people had ever stepped into before. There were tigers, orangutans—the whole deal. Back at the camp, and when we went on leave in Singapore: big decadent parties, rich Westerners running roughshod over local values. A genuinely exotic, strange world—and it was really something to be in there not as a journalist/interloper but as an authentic member of the community.

Likewise later, when I worked for a pharmaceutical company and an environmental engineering firm back home, it was entry into a restricted world. If a person has any feelings about power and corporations (I do), what a great chance to see that beast from the inside. It complicated my moral vision, this chance to see people I knew and liked (including me) participating in things that were iffy—to see the way we justified these things in real time and made them square with our ideas of ourselves as good people. So these work experiences had the effect of politicizing me from the gut. To be on the Oppressor side of the table, to participate in rich narcissistic excesses in the midst of real poverty—to walk, drunk at midnight, past a construction site where 150 elderly Singaporean women were manually lugging big boulders out of an excavation—it made clear, even to a young dunderhead like I was, that whatever good and evil are, they're real, and it's within our power to distinguish between the two.

Many have claimed that your work evidences a deep commitment to ethics of morality, justice, and responsibility. How do you view your own work? Is there a sense of morality that you feel imbues what you create?

Well, I think the only morality in a story is to not be boring. Any other intention is going to get gummy and preachy because it assumes that Author knows, Reader doesn't, which is a big snore. But "don't be boring" is complicated. How might we avoid being boring? Well, for one thing, by avoiding condescension. How do we avoid condescension? By taking everything into account. By crediting our reader with full intelligence. By giving our characters something that feels like agency. By knowing enough about the real world that the stories we tell aren't trivial or masturbatory. So, in a sense, all of these aesthetic imperatives add up to *something like* a moral imperative.

If we could actually abide by all of these, we would make a fictional world that amounts to an accurate rhetorical model of the real one that asks the right questions, formulates them correctly, credits opposing impulses—all of which, I think, tends to *feel* moral. But for me, it's important to go back to the basics: keep the reader engaged via some sort of charm. Otherwise, your story might do that most deadly thing: put the reader to sleep, or cause her to close the book and go outside.

Can you recall any moments when you felt particularly discouraged as a writer? What helped to sustain your belief in your work and in yourself on these occasions?

There were certainly times where I should have felt discouraged, but even at those low points, I was arrogant or hopeful or deluded enough to put the bad news behind me pretty quickly, I think. I once wrote a 700-page book about a Mexican wedding of a friend of mine, which was called *La Boda de Eduardo*. Roughly translated: *Ed's Wedding*. Enough said. That one took about a year of work and lots of late nights at a time when we had a new baby at home and I was working full time. So when it turned out to suck, that was hard. But in my heart, I think I knew it sucked, so it was also kind of a relief—to find out I was right regarding the sucking and that my taste was still active, so to speak. And also a relief to put that book (or *libro*, as I might have called it back then) behind me and move onto something more worthwhile and... alive.

There is something so wonderful about writing in a way that feels new and authentic, that feels in line with your true taste—trying to get to that place is like seeking the Grail. Whatever hardships have to be endured along the way are fine—part of the larger quest, if you will. Although, I didn't feel that way the day after *La Boda de Eduardo* went in El Garbago.

Can you describe your view of the purpose of writing?

I think there are a lot of reasons to read and to write, and that anyone who's ever read or written knows what they are. So this question of purpose which, I think, all writers obsess over might just be a little celebratory thing we do at the end of the day—a dog on a porch wagging its tail. There is the usual stable of answers (all of which I believe, by the way): reading opens a person up, makes him more aware; is an axe to crack the frozen sea within us; does not solve problems, only formulates them correctly; makes a person more compassionate, by letting her into someone else's mind. All of those are true—but none are sufficient. Does writing fight evil? If so, how? Yes, I think it can, but a little bit at a time, in much the same way that a small act of kindness might or a good song. And a quick survey of the last 500 years will tell us that if writing does fight evil, it's not doing such a crackerjack job of it. Although, on the other hand, to really know, you'd have to scroll out the last 500 years without any writing or reading in it... gads! (Although, on the other, other hand, that would take *Mein Kampf* out of the world, along with gazillion other hysterical tracts...)

I once had someone use one of my stories to justify doing a pretty crappy thing, and since then, I've had a different feeling about the "writing does good" thing. Because "a read" is an intersection of story plus reader—and who can predict how that's going to come out, or what it might lead to? A person could read Chekhov's "Gooseberries"—a beautiful meditation on, among many other things, what we might call "the evil of happiness"—and conclude: Exterminate the bourgeoisie brutes.

As I think is true with anything worth dedicating your life to, the real pleasures and benefits of writing are beyond logic and reduction. Most writers do it, I think, because it's fun and they're good at it and it gets them some power in the world and—like a little possible side benefit—may have some positive micro-effects. But I don't think we should confuse writing with goodness or positive causation. Writing can be imbued with spiritual virtues: kindness, truth, accuracy, complexity, etc., etc., but not all writing is. Maybe all good writing is, but even there, I think you have to be careful. One thing good writing is, is beautiful. That is, it gives some pleasure. In the end, that might be what I really believe about writing: it can be honed into something non-random and strangely moving—and we don't know why.

What was one of the most challenging writing endeavors you undertook and why?

I spent a week in a homeless camp in Fresno and wrote about that for GQ. That was challenging for a lot of reasons, not the least of which was the gap between what I thought I'd find (a bunch of Steinbeck characters) and what I actually found (a group of mentally ill and/or addicted and/or violent people living in what was essentially a crack house, or, to be more accurate, two competing crack houses). It was very intense as an experience and equally intense to try and do some justice to all that comedy and heartbreak when I got home and tried to write about it.

Which authors and books have motivated your own journey as a writer and your commitment to crafting fiction?

In roughly chronological order: Esther Forbes, Ernest Hemingway, Thomas Wolfe, Jack Kerouac, Stuart Dybek, Raymond Carver, Tobias Wolff, Isaac Babel, Kurt Vonnegut, Barry Hannah, Toni Morrison, Anton Chekhov, Nikolai Gogol, Leo Tolstoy. Some important books were: *In Our Time, Visions of Gerard, Airships, Red Cavalry, The Coast of Chicago, In the Garden of the North American Martyrs, Cathedral, Catch-22,* and various stories by Gogol ("The Nose," "The Overcoat") and Tolstoy ("Master and Man," and "Alyosha the Pot") and Chekhov (especially the "About Love" trilogy). That's far from a complete list, of course. I was also influenced by comedians, mainly Steve Martin, Monty Python, WC Fields, and the Marx Brothers.

What inspires you to craft prose, and what deflates you (if anything)?

It just feels like a natural urge. Especially once I have some prose in front of me, the urge to improve it is very strong. I have very specific taste in sentences, I think, so when confronted with one, I almost always have an opinion on it, which leads to edits, which leads to a new version, which leads to edits— and soon the moon is coming up.

Were there any formative moments from your childhood that you would say uniquely prepared you for the vocation / career of a writer?

We were a storytelling and joke-telling family, so I think I got the message early that language equals power. Also, a nun gave me the book *Johnny Tremain* when I was in third grade, and the combination of the tightness of the language and the fact that I had a crush on this particular nun made for a "formative moment," which was roughly, if I could write like this, that nun would love me.

Can you share a particularly difficult rejection story and how you overcame the emotion of that experience?

Honestly, as I look back at myself as a young writer, I'm struck by how unemotional I was about rejection. I mean, I hated it, but my low self-esteem always made me think, when rejected, *Duh, of course, they're completely right.* But then another thing would kick in, which was a strong urge to get back to the drawing board and get it right this time. Often when I was getting rejected, I didn't have one-hundred percent positive feelings about the piece anyway—I'd done my best but didn't feel that real pull of connection to the piece that I now think is diagnostic of "being done." So it didn't feel like it was *me* getting rejected—just that flawed thing I had made and felt ambivalent about. Nowadays, when rejected, it maybe hurts a little more—now it feels like I have something to lose, and it can feel a little embarrassing, but that goes away pretty quickly. And a good stiff rejection almost always has the effect of making my standards for the piece go up. I can usually, right away, see things I should have seen before sending it out.

Can you share the story of your first publication (book, article, or otherwise) and what that experience was like—any emotions, contemplations, or lessons associated with it?

Well, those kinds of successes are like any successes or bits of good fortune, both wonderful and somehow... not enough. I remember real pleasures—getting the finished book or magazine in the mail or whatever... but also, then, a feeling of, "Darn, it would appear that all my neuroses have not magically disappeared as I'd hoped they would!" Likewise, "And my ambition still seems intact! Ditto my ego! Ditto my feeling that, if only I could accomplish something, I would be more comfortable in my skin!" So then you write another book. As they say on the shampoo bottles, "Rinse, lather, repeat." The trick seems to be to get into some kind of relationship with that cycle of (a) wanting to write a book, (b) writing a book, (c) having written a book, (d) wanting to write (another) book, etc., etc. Happiness has to be found in there somewhere, apart from the success or failure of the venture.

Michelle Wildgen

etting her literary start as an intern at the prestigious *Tin House* magazine, Wildgen is now Executive Editor there. She earned an MFA in Creative Writing from Sarah Lawrence College. Working in the dual roles of editor and author, Wildgen conveys a host of wisdom from both experiences and offers keen insight on how she keeps these roles separate. Her list of publications includes the novels *You're Not You* (Picador, 2007) and *But Not for Long* (Picador, 2007). Additionally, Wildgen has edited the volume, *Food and Booze: A Tin House Literary Feast* (Tin House Books, 2006).

You're Not You came out of a short story you wrote. Can you describe the process of making your story into a novel—its delights and despairs, and how the eventual work compares to your original vision for the story?

I expanded the story into the first half or so of the novel rather than building all around it, so a lot of the early work was figuring out what required or would benefit from expansion without becoming slack. The first draft was just a skeleton, about a hundred pages long, but it gave me the pieces to move around, and after that, I just kept going back to the beginning and revising. By far the hardest part of the process was the very beginning. No matter how many stories I'd written, I felt paralyzed facing a novel, as if I'd never even read one. Where to start? Broad scope, small pointillist moment? I rewrote those first sixty pages many, many times, trying to get them moving briskly while still establishing the characters' lives. Some things changed from story to novel—characters had more room to be complex, I hope, names changed, Bec's age changed, I think. Just changes that seemed necessary when I was re-envisioning the story from a later perspective and based on what I'd gotten to know about them.

*Besides your work as a novelist, you are also the Executive Editor of the thriving literary magazine, **Tin House**. How do you balance the work for each pursuit, and do your roles ever play off one another to spur on your ideas for crafting fiction?*

Tin House is not full time for me, which helps a lot. I also sometimes teach or freelance edit or write, whatever comes up, because I do like having a variety of pursuits and don't think I could write eight hours a day even if money were no object. The downside is that sometimes writing gets shoved to the back behind better-paying pursuits or behind a bottleneck of projects. Which isn't my favorite thing, but what can you do? I have to earn money, too, after all.

I do find that writing and editing are very separate things for me. I have learned a lot from editing that I hope I apply in writing—such as knowing that, no, editors do not care about the first twelve pages of a story in which nothing happens, no matter how pretty the writing—and certainly editing has helped me approach submitting my work in a much calmer way. I spend so much time rejecting stories that go on to find good homes that I don't feel as demoralized as I used to when I get a rejection. But when generating work, I keep the two separate, and writing requires me to forget all about the possibility of sending out the work at some point. I can't get the necessary space if I'm already imagining the editorial response to a narrative I'm just figuring out.

Can you recall any moments when you felt particularly discouraged as a writer? What helped to sustain your belief in your work and in yourself on these occasions?

There have been plenty; there continue to be plenty. I've gotten agent rejections and grad school rejections and publisher rejections, and I have certainly had those moments when I think, *There must be something really fundamentally crappy about my work if it is as easy as it appears to be for people to pass it by.* Or there are the times when I feel like there are so many writers, so few of whom really reach readers. Everyone is striving yet all these books just disappear, and it can all feel a little Sisyphean.

What gets me through that is writing and ignoring it. It's the writing I enjoy, the accomplishment of generating work, and accepting that, to some extent, this process is the only one I really, really care about. My goal was never to be rich and famous. It was and is to write well. I'll write as long as I find it gratifying and compelling.

What do you love most about the life of a writer?

I love the fact that reading great books counts as work for me. I love the feeling of having made something from nothing. I love the way your own work surprises you, as if someone else wrote it, when it is going well, and the bizarre and fascinating ways the brain connects emotions and nuances in fiction that I'd never have come to if I just sat down and mapped it all out. Those weird synchronicities of world building might be my favorite thing.

Least?

The whole marketing thing, everyone trying to reach readers through the same few channels, and my own deficiencies at that process. There are exceptions, but by and large, I think it's fair to say that most writers, being people who are fine spending many hours alone, are not natural extroverts and marketers at heart, but we have to try to be, and it's not always a comfortable fit. Writing and publishing are two vastly different things; both necessary, obviously, though I much prefer the writing.

Which authors and books have motivated your own journey as a writer and your commitment to crafting fiction?

When I was a teenager I fell in love with Ann Beattie's work, so that was big. I didn't really get what she was doing, but that didn't stop me from imitating it. And Laurie Colwin's writing is still a huge favorite: witty, comic but not lightweight, plus plenty of food in there, which I love. MFK Fisher's food writing knocked me out when I first encountered it: this is not "how to make a nice casserole with your leftovers," but food as the canvas for family, marriage, sex, death, and disappointment. Alice Munro seems able to do almost anything, enter a story from any point in time, layer on the perspectives, write about people who are far from energetic and exciting and cosmopolitan and yet make them riveting.

In your work as an editor, what strikes you most and resonates in reading submissions?

Freshness! We see a lot of stories, and I want to see some new layer in there—in the voice, in the emotional response of the characters to what might be a familiar situation, something.

The biggest reason I end up passing on perfectly sound work is that it held no surprises for me, what I thought would happen did, characters did just as we have seen characters do before and for the same reasons. I want the characters to be as varied and unexpected as if I grabbed someone off the street and started asking them about their lives. Without that kind of energy, what makes one story stand out from a thousand others? That said, this is one of the most subjective aspects of reading submissions: what I am thoroughly unmoved by will be profound for someone else and vice versa. Another reason you can't get too hung up on rejections is that sometimes, you have to find your reader.

Do you keep any rules for yourself when it comes to writing? Can you share any of the kinds of daily disciplines you use to help you continue crafting new work?

It varies depending on what my writing and working life look like at the moment. As long as I am mentally in a project, I can approach it in varying ways and feel productive: I might be writing a few afternoons a week, or more or less. It does help to transition from whatever mundane tasks I was doing to writing, often by reading a few pages from a great book to get me back in that mindset. I find it very hard to just finish lunch, sit down, and say, "And now I compose."

Daniel Handler (a.k.a. Lemony Snicket)

I first heard Daniel Handler speak (as Lemony Snicket's representative) at the Northern Arizona Book Festival in 2007. In a word, I was mesmerized. Handler's irresistible charm of the audience is similar to the aura that has endeared readers of the bestselling saga, *A Series of Unfortunate Events*. However, Handler also writes adult literary fiction. He is the author of two novels: *Watch Your Mouth* (Ecco, 2002) and *The Basic Eight* (Harper Perennial, 2006); and the short story collection *Adverbs* (Ecco, 2007). He shares here his early love affair with writing, the experience of a bizarre rejection, and what he loves most about making words.

How did you feel when your remarkable A Series of Unfortunate Events books became part of nearly everyone's daily diction? What were some of the highs and lows associated with this rare experience?

The experience hasn't been "high" or "low;" it's been strange. It is strange to disembark a plane on a faraway continent and have complete strangers dressing up like characters I've invented. It's strange to have the problem of a signing at a bookstore lasting too long. It's strange to go on television and talk with a perfectly straight face about a secret organization. It's strange to go onto a movie set and be told I cannot enter a door marked "Lemony Snicket." Everything about what has happened to me is strange, and the strangeness has not worn off.

You write in two different genres — literary fiction for adults and fiction for middle graders and YAs. How do you find the energy for both, and what first got you interested in writing for each audience?

I don't get interested in writing for a particular audience; I get interested in telling a particular story. Sometimes the story falls under the umbrella of children's literature, which I see as more of a genre than a category of readership. After all, many people who aren't children read children's literature, just as many children read my other books.

What about writing do you most enjoy?

Everything about writing but word processing software.

What keeps you writing when you really (really!) don't feel like it?

I always feel like writing. Sometimes I don't feel like writing the specific thing I'm writing, but I usually keep at it anyway, on the grounds that five pages of nonsense is more likely to produce a workable sentence than not doing anything. A brisk walk sometimes helps, as does listening to recordings by The Flying Lizards.

Are there ever stages or moments during the course of your writing life when you feel like quitting? If so, what keeps you at it? If not, why do you figure your heart wouldn't let your mind think about throwing in the towel?

I have a narrative mind, so when I imagine stopping writing, I try to think of what comes next. Nothing does that brings me any pleasure. Of course, on a daily basis, I think about stopping around three o'clock in the afternoon, and I do, while the rest of the working world fakes it for another couple of hours. This brings me pleasure.

What makes you belly laugh?

The *Mr. Show* skit about the thimble collection.

What makes you fake laugh?

People's stories of how they got engaged.

When you read someone else's work, what makes you say, Holy Crap! That is remarkable!

The sucker punch of the casual and the searingly true.

Can you share a particularly difficult rejection story and how you overcame the emotion of that experience?

Once an editor called me, having read my first and then-unpublished novel, and said she wanted to take me to dinner. Over dinner she told me she had no interest in publishing the book, but was just curious to lay eyes on me. Rejected, broke, desperate, I walked home from dinner towards my unaffordable apartment where my wife was waiting in suspense. Feeling very sorry for myself, I detoured to a bar and ordered a bourbon. The woman asked me how I wanted it. Unable to think of the word *neat*, I said, "in a glass." She laughed and told me it was a good line, and I realized I was still a writer.

Can you share the story of your first publication (book, article, or otherwise) and what that experience was like—any emotions, contemplations, or lessons associated with it?

It wasn't quite the first thing I published, but when I was twenty-three, my then-girlfriend-now-wife and I started a 'zine called *American Chickens!* I have a very clear memory of standing at a Kinko's making copies of it, and when Lisa folded up the first copy, we stood together and read it and were howling with laughter right there in the middle of the place. Nobody ever loved that 'zine the way we did, of course, but I knew then I wanted to do something that brought me that kind of joy for the rest of my life.

Olugbemisola Rhuday-Perkovich

With her debut novel, *Eighth Grade Superzero* (Arthur A. Levine / Scholastic, 2010) released to wide critical acclaim, Rhuday-Perkovich accomplished something few novelists can manage. She crafted a novel that is at once moving, vivid, and gripping, and which also has a poignant social conscience and the example of a protagonist who is believably authentic and still completely interested in changing the world around him for better—not just in his own journey, but in the bigger journey, too. *Publisher's Weekly* gave the book a coveted starred review and it was also chosen as an Amazon Best Books of the Month pick for January of 2010.

Rhuday-Perkovich is an author known not only for her stellar writing, but for her meaningful work as an activist as well. One need only explore her website,

http://www.olugbemisolabooks.com/ ,

to see the incredible opportunities she presents and the experiences of world changing that she shares. Here, she shares a huge dose of encouragement, book recommendations, and telling insights from her own journey.

How did the idea for Eighth Grade Superzero first come to you?

It started as part of an application for a writing workshop with Paula Danziger, whose work I'd loved dearly since childhood. It was one of those night-before-the-application was due kind of things (a situation that I find myself in often), and I wasn't going to pass up a chance to be in the same room with her for a week! I got an image of my main character, Reggie, in my head and went with it for three pages. He appeared as a 10-year-old boy hiding under the covers in his bed, afraid of bugs and terrified of being laughed at. I knew that he'd thrown up in front of everyone on the first day of school and was tormented by his older sister. That was about it for a while, those three pages. Over a four year period, Reggie grew and bloomed, and we got to know each other well. It was through his relationships with his friends that I really came to love and understand him.

Can you share details of your journey to create that novel, from idea to seeing it on bookshelves? What were some of the greatest highs and the lowest lows (if any) along the journey?

I'd gotten to a point where I told myself that I had to stop "wanting to be" a writer, or being afraid to think of myself as a writer, and just… write. And keep going. The keeping going part was hard. I spend a lot of time thinking about characters and making random notes that are not part of the story. I need to really know my characters in order to know how their stories go, but I think that I can also use that as an excuse to avoid letting the story progress. I got stuck many times in a rut of revising the same chapters over and over, trying to make them "perfect." I was fortunate enough to have had some workshops with the wonderful Madeleine L'Engle, who told me to STOP TRYING TO BE A PERFECTIONIST because I'd never get anything done, and that was some of the best advice I've ever gotten. Once I remind myself that it won't be perfect on the first, second, third, or gazillionth try—or really, ever—I can relax and just try to do the best I can to tell the story with honesty and love. But oh, I do have to remind myself of that every. Single. Day. One of the biggest highs was getting an e-mail only a week after I'd queried an editor (Cheryl Klein, at Arthur A. Levine/ Scholastic), saying, "Can I see the rest?" I did squeal and jump up and down. Then I panicked because I had no "rest" to send just yet. I spent the next week feverishly writing!

Your work has been honored for its focus on activism. Do you see intersections for writing and activism, and if so, where might they be?

As I began to seek out Reggie's real story, I was inspired by people and moments in my life, and some of the teens that I taught and worked with—their desire to tackle big questions, to be thoughtful, and to be activists in many different ways. I do think writing and activism certainly intersect in a variety of ways. I was taught from a very young age about "the power of the pen," from simple petitions to letter writing and opinion writing—and my family always held fast to the power of stories to give voice and shape to a desire for justice and as an avenue to doing our part to make the world a better place.

I hope that my readers connect with the idea that there are many different kinds of "heroes," many ways to be an activist. I hope that readers know that the small things they do matter, and not everything that we say, do, and think needs to be for public consumption or for some sort of recognition. And there is always room for mercy, redemption, and growth. I hope that they're inspired to make things, without worrying about being good at it. And I hope that they challenge themselves, willing to be uncomfortable regularly. And "walk the rocky hillside, sowing clover," as Wendell Berry wrote.

How are you supported as a writer, and what keeps you motivated to continue working on new projects?

I'm fascinated by people, by the small moments, and the big what ifs... I'm inspired and buoyed through my faith, by my fantastic family and friends, by the children and teens that I meet... I have always needed to write, and always will—it's my way of growing and working out what I think, figuring out my place in the world, sharing a bit of myself with others.

If someone sat down with you for lunch and shared that their dream was to publish a middle grade novel, what might you share with them by way of advice?

Read. Read. Read some more. Keep writing. Don't give up. Listen well, and revise with attention to the *story* and not necessarily your technique or your intent. Don't take *yourself* too seriously, but give your work the love and respect it deserves.

What disciplines help you stay focused and creative as a writer?

Sometimes, I design my own "workshop" by reading books like Peter Turchi's *Maps of the Imagination*, Francine Prose's *Reading Like a Writer*, Marita Golden's *The Word*, and James Wood's *How Fiction Works*. Anne Lamott's *Bird by Bird* and Anne Morrow Lindbergh's *Gift from the Sea* are beloved in my home library as well. Recently, I've gotten into the practice of story-boarding books that I admire, which is enormously helpful. A critique partner and/or "accountability" partner is essential, especially for a loner like me; it's so good to have trusted author friends with whom I can discuss books, writing, etc., and be inspired, get unstuck, or just remember the wonderfulness of this work that we do.

I drink lots and lots of tea, strong, black, and sweet, (like me—heh). I "walk-write" a lot—I work out scenes, parts of the stories that are challenging me, or come up with ideas while I walk. (I usually walk very early in the morning so that fewer people see me talking and gesturing to myself.) I tend to have public radio on while I work at home, and I still write my notes and first drafts in longhand. It works a different part of my brain and adds another level of revision to my writing. I *love* to revise. It's those first drafts that just about destroy me. I try to write something every day, even if it ends up being just a page of X's. I believe in keeping the pen moving. Usually something, some "cosmos out of chaos" (a term I learned from Madeleine) will come.

Can you share the story of your first publication (book, article, or otherwise) and what that experience was like—any emotions, contemplations, or lessons associated with it?

I think my first "official" published piece was when I was in college; it was an article for the *Ithaca Times*. I covered my school's "State of Black America" conference for the paper, and it was a real thrill to see it in print! A close friend had that article framed and surprised me with that soon after it had been published. I can't say enough how much the love and support of my family and friends throughout my writing life has meant to me.

Can you share a list of your favorite works, or works that inspire you deeply?

My parents gave me such a gift during my childhood and teen years. They offered a lot of freedom to browse library shelves and choose my own books. It was wonderful to be around a family of readers… to be in a family that valued literacy. Books were a place of respite for me during a tough time; they gave me a space to work out who I was, even try on different identities at times.

Some of my childhood favorites that I still have are *Where the Sidewalk Ends* by Shel Silverstein and a pile of Nancy Drew mysteries. *I Know Why the Caged Bird Sings, The Autobiography of Malcolm X,* and *Anne Frank: Diary of a Young Girl* were books that I read when I was too young to understand them fully, but I "got" something; they resonated with me in a major way. Madeleine L'Engle's books—*A Wrinkle in Time, A Wind in the Door,* and *A Ring of Endless Light* were very precious to me. My mom read *Wrinkle* aloud to me during a year that we lived in Lagos, and that was a wonderful time. Those books helped me reflect on death, grieving… imperfect heroines… the different ways we learn to love. Around that time, I also collected the "African Writers Series," and just had a real thirst for "regular" stories about Africans and their daily lives, and enjoyed books by Cyprian Ekwensi and Buchi Emecheta. Chinua Achebe's *No Longer at Ease* was devastating and told a story about relationship to homeland that resonated with me even then.

Their Eyes Were Watching God was big for me as a teen. In high school, I worked on a term paper on Zora Neale Hurston, and our school librarian told me repeatedly that there was no such person when I asked for research help. That really reinforced my decision to take responsibility for my own education—and to seek out well-informed librarians, because of course, there are loads of them! I was also blessed during junior high and high school with two great teachers, Ms. Glover and Ms. Anderson, who were committed to educating all of their students about the Black experience across the Diaspora, not as something exotic or foreign, but something that mattered. They really challenged us in terms of critical reading and artistic expression.

I loved folk tales, fairy tales, and myths. The collections by Julius Lester and Virginia Hamilton, I adored. *Till We Have Faces* by C.S. Lewis is one of my all-time favorites. The line "how can we expect the gods to meet us face to face till we have faces" captures what intrigued me most about this story of a young princess who becomes a true princess. I was a young woman who believed, on the pages of my journals, that I was a hidden princess.

Some others: *The Cat Ate My Gymsuit*, a classic novel of a teenage girl really digging deep to uncover her voice. *Pride and Prejudice*, because Elizabeth had sass and could face her mistakes with dignity. (Plus, I was OBSESSED with becoming "an accomplished woman").

It was also during the teen years that I learned to read critically. For instance, I was a huge Agatha Christie fan (she does tight, neat description so well), but also began to look more closely at the racist and/or anti-Semitic sentiments that were present in those and other favorites. It also became clear that it wasn't much fun so often seeing people of color in literature as "problems" to be dealt with or ignored.

Much later, I read Bell Hooks' essay on "writing auto-biography" as a way of "talking back." I've always loved memoir. I was always talking back as a reader, and my writing is a way of talking back (and much easier for me than say, actual talking!). I don't know what I'd have done, or what I'd do now, without books and stories. I love to reread those old favorites, and I'm transformed every time. I always wanted to write, and did always write in some form, and I think that in writing for children I'd love to give just a small shadow of the gifts that I got from books during those years.

What most irks you and delights you about the enterprise of getting a book published in today's business?

I love the community building that can happen today with the use of Internet technology; that's been invaluable. New technology also means that there are more types of "reading" competing for readers' attention, so the industry sometimes seems less willing to innovate, to take chances on new writers, with storytelling traditions other than Western ones, etc. It really remains difficult for authors of color who want to work within the traditional publishing system to tell *all* of our stories, *all* of our truths. And again, new technology—the growth of independent publishing, community building that can form author cooperatives and new business models is a large part of what will change that.

No matter what happens in the industry, I will always delight in the power of story. Our stories matter, our stories are precious, and each and every one of our stories is beautiful in its own lovely and amazing way.

Jane Smiley

An inductee into the American Academy of Arts and Letters in 2001, Jane Smiley is a writer of prodigious wisdom, work, and energy. After winning the Pulitzer Prize for her 1991 novel *A Thousand Acres*, Smiley continued to craft critically praised novels like *Good Faith* (Knopf, 2003) and *Ten Days in the Hills* (Anchor, 2008). Smiley shares her deep love of writing and how her early successes and rejections influenced her growth. In addition to her numerous novels, Smiley also writes for publications such as *The New Yorker*, *The Practical Horseman*, *Vogue*, and *The Nation*, among others. Her massive work of literary criticism, *13 Ways of Looking at the Novel* (Knopf, 2005), and her biography of Charles Dickens (Viking, 2002), reveal two other genres in which Smiley has worked. In 2006, she was honored with the PEN USA Lifetime Achievement Award for Literature.

*I once read that, years after the publication of **A Thousand Acres**, you felt as though you would have liked to change elements of the book. Does that sense come out of the editor in you, or the fact that your perception as a writer has changed, or from elsewhere?*

I changed my analysis of the composition of *King Lear* by WS, from a conviction that he was on Lear's side and condemning the daughters as a man and a father might to a different idea. I discovered at a Shakespeare conference that Shakespeare's father may have suffered from dementia. I came to see the daughters as three parts of his reaction to the old man — two parts cruel and one part compassionate. That answered, for me, why the daughters are so flat and why, in some sense, Lear has no past as a King with a history of various wars, policies, etc. But I don't think I wanted to change *A Thousand Acres* because a book as a whole and grows out of a conception. To change the conception is to write a different book.

What is the most enjoyable part of the writing process for you?

Making stuff up.

The most dreaded part of the writing process (if you have one)?

Having to make stuff up. But usually one little mote of an idea is enough to get me going, and then it gets enjoyable.

What keeps you writing when you really (really!) don't feel like it?

I am not in the habit of not feeling like it. I'm used to it. I know I will enjoy having done it. An addiction is something that you really want to do but makes you feel horrible afterwards. A passion is something that maybe you are reluctant to begin but feels wonderful afterwards. For me, writing is a career, an activity, a habit, and a passion.

How has success (becoming a bestselling author and winning numerous prestigious prizes) affected you as a writer? Does it relate at all to the way you work, craft scenes, and your goals?

I don't know. However, since I was already in the habit of writing before those things happened, they were more like glancing blows than formative experiences. Also, I've always lived on the periphery, so I haven't really experienced fame (or notoriety) on a daily basis. Horses don't care what you write, and most horse people don't, either.

What are some of the purposes for writing as you see it?

Exploration! Earning a living (if you are lucky). Developing whole thoughts. Setting words next to one another so that they pop.

Can you share a particularly difficult rejection story and how you overcame the emotion of that experience?

My best friend was my editor until *Duplicate Keys*. We started out together, enjoyed one another, and got along editorially. Her boss wouldn't buy *Duplicate Keys*, so we were forcibly divorced. I ended up at Knopf, and we are still best friends, so it turned out okay. I did panic and I did get quite upset, but I do love Knopf...

Can you share the story of your first publication (book, article, or otherwise) and what that experience was like—any emotions, contemplations, or lessons associated with it?

I don't remember the first ones very well, but I do remember what a wonderful feeling it was to get a big check for selling a story to a popular magazine. I think the 1200 dollar check was equivalent to two months' salary. I was pretty amazed and happy. My favorite publication story took place about nine years later, in 1986. I had two little girls, one eight and one four. I was getting them ready for school and day care early in the morning, and they were very uncooperative and cranky. The phone rang as I was trying to hurry them out the door. I think I answered it rather impatiently. It was *The Atlantic* buying "The Blinding Light of the Mind" for a major sum. I turned to the girls and said, "Quick, you can have anything you want!" The eight-year-old chose a doll and the four-year-old a stuffed animal. And we were all happy! They jumped in the car, and I took them to school. That was a great morning.

Robert Pinsky

First honored as Poet Laureate of the United States in 1997, Pinsky has been a passionate advocate for poetry that meets and affects people in their daily walks of life. His publications include a plethora of poetic volumes, the first of which was published in 1975 by Princeton University Press under the title *Sadness and Happiness*. His collections include *Jersey Rain* (2000) and *Gulf Music* (2007), both published by Farrar, Strauss, and Giroux. He has also written volumes of criticism and edited the work and collections of other poets. Most recently, the former Poet Laureate has published *Selected Poems* (Farrar Straus and Giroux, 2011). He has also just released a CD with pianist Laurence Hobgood, called POEMJAZZ from Circumstantial Productions. Pinsky responded to my questions with enthusiastic compliance, and in an evening's quick reply articulates the need for writers to be continually moved and inspired by language—its power and beauty.

Growing up, were there any experiences that you see as formative to your journey as a writer? Or, in a broader scope, how do you see childhood contributing to (or hindering?) the work of a writer?

There may be a peculiar advantage to having failed: D or F in some courses in eighth and ninth grade, never doing very well in high school. I think I gained a little detachment and maybe some useful fatalism from that. At the same time, I was sustained by playing music; music gave me a social identity and absorbing work. So, an art was at the center of my life and my imagination, while official recognition was not. Music (along with aptitude tests, IQ tests, College Boards, all that kind of thing) saved me.

Robert Herrick in the 17th century advises, "To Live Merrily and Trust to Good Verses." That's an ambition I can embrace.

What keeps you writing when you really (really!) don't feel like it?

I only work when I feel like it. That may be another legacy (or continuation?) of early failure. On the other hand, I quite often feel like it—maybe in a spirit of compensation? In a way, that sense of failure or incapacity *makes* me feel like it.

So, I complain, I kvetch, I lament that I cannot get to work, I moan that I cannot get anything done—but those are ways to occupy myself until I feel like it.

How has success (being named Poet Laureate, receiving National fellowships and awards) affected you as a writer? Does it relate at all to the way you work?

I believe in concentrating on accomplishment, not success.

On a daily level, you can see and measure success and recognition, while you can never be certain of accomplishment. John Keats's epitaph for himself is, "Here lies one whose name was writ in water."

But on the deepest, truest level, accomplishment is real. Success and recognition are matters of opinion.

What are some of the purposes for writing as you see it?

In the video segments at www.favoritepoem.org, I find the

purpose of writing for me. I'd like to make a poem that another person wants to say aloud as Seph Rodney says Sylvia Plath's poem, or the young Marine says Yeats's poem, or the construction worker says lines by Whitman.

A young poet comes to you, sheaves of paper in hand, distraught and on the border of giving up. She loves poetry but struggles to find a way to keep writing in the midst of so much rejection. What might you tell her?

Go back to the poetry that most inspires you, your favorite lines by Dickinson or Hopkins or whatever instilled a love of the art in you. Type out that poetry or write it longhand, then memorize it. Read the letters of Keats or Chekhov, or whoever inspires you. Only your love of the art can sustain you amid the oblivious or unjust qualities of the world.

Allen Ginsberg, at the end of "A Supermarket in California," addresses Walt Whitman as "lonely old courage-teacher." Find your courage-teachers, and honor them by reading their work as you hope someone will read yours.

Kathryn Erskine

Winner of the National Book Award for Young People's Literature in 2010, Kathryn Erskine's work deals with deeply important themes. *Mockingbird* (Philomel / Penguin 2010), which won her the NBA, explores life through the eyes of a young girl with Asperger's Syndrome who tries to nurture her family, her school, and her town back to strength after a school shooting. Her novel, *The Absolute Value of Mike* (Philomel / Penguin, 2011), reveals the life of a young boy who must learn his own worth even as his father can't seem to see the genuine strength of his son. In the process of living apart during a summer, Mike comes to learn his own power when it's tested and needed to sustain a community with real problems, real needs.

Erskine's life is defined by unique cultural experiences, including an eclectic mix of locales where she grew from childhood to an adult, such as the Netherlands, Israel, South Africa, Scotland, and Canada. She now resides in Virginia and writes everything from picture books to novels. Her work—like her life—is characterized by hope in the face of anything, belief in the good, and the value of working towards peace.

When did you first decide that you wanted to be a writer, and what was the journey like to be able to fully claim and believe that for yourself?

I always loved writing but thought I'd write once I retired. When my mom died, still in her sixties, I realized that I should follow my passion *now* because you never know what's going to happen. My mom was an excellent writer but never had a book published. I decided I wanted to realize that goal for myself.

What is the most enjoyable part of the writing process for you?

Definitely the creative surge, when your writing or typing can't keep up with the ideas pouring out of your head, when you're laughing at your own jokes, or saying "Yes! That's perfect!" as new ideas keep coming and coming.

The most dreaded part of the writing process (if you have one)?

I used to dread revisions but now I see that phase as a second chance, a fresh look, an opportunity to improve what I've written. It's the business side of the work that's draining for me: I love the trips and events, but the planning and logistics of those trips and events are a chore.

What keeps you writing when you really (really!) don't feel like it?

Usually, I'm eager to write, but if I'm stressed or distracted by other things in my life, it can be very hard. I have a lot of reasons to keep going, though—the sacrifices we make so I can stay home and write, the unfailing support of my husband, the eyes of my children since I want to be a good role model, and letters from readers who tell me how much one of my books means to them.

How has success (becoming a bestselling author and winning the National Book Award for Mockingbird) affected you as a writer? Does it relate at all to the way you work, craft scenes, and your goals?

Mostly, I try not to think about it, except that it does ratchet up expectations so I really want to write something worthwhile. The difficulty is finding enough time to write, given the amount of time and energy I spend on the road or Skyping or blogging or any writing-related activity that's not actually writing.

What are some of the purposes for writing as you see it?

Many—everything from self-expression and self-exploration to connecting with others to sharing knowledge to, most importantly in my opinion, helping others, especially young people, by giving them a helping hand; laughter; some happiness; and most of all, hope.

Can you share a particularly difficult rejection story and how you overcame the emotion of that experience?

I must've blocked them all because I can't think of any, although I've received lots of rejections! I do remember a funny one, though. I received a poorly photocopied letter from a publishing house in response to my manuscript. In fact, it was a part of a letter because the bottom part had been roughly torn off, and it began with the usual "it's lovely BUT" language, so I threw it in the trash. My husband was appalled that I hadn't even finished reading the letter so he fished it out of the trash and read it… and it was a request for the rest of the manuscript! In the end, they didn't buy it anyway, but it was a good lesson to read the complete letter even if it looks like a shoddy form rejection.

Can you share the story of your first publication (book, article, or otherwise) and what that experience was like—any emotions, contemplations, or lessons associated with it?

I think the publication of *Quaking* (2007) with the first large, traditional publishing house (Penguin) was the most exciting. It was a long process (years) getting to that point and many revisions, so when I received the bound ARC's, the paperback version of the book-to-be, I was elated. It finally felt real. I was holding the book in my hand. It was actually going to happen. My book was being published. It seemed to take forever to get to that point—even when the manuscript was complete, it was going to be a year or more before it was actually published. That's the time you want to brainstorm who might be interested in the book, where you could speak, what contacts you have, which kinds of promotional items you want to order (I highly recommend temporary tattoos of the book jacket), and everything else you can think of to prepare. It'll help fill the time which drags so slo-o-o-owly. And then everything happens. It really does. So hang in there and keep writing!

David Wroblewski

G rowing up in rural Wisconsin, Wroblewski fell in love with stories early on, and his curiosity about how a novel is crafted and how a story unfolds eventually led him to enroll in the Warren Wilson MFA program for Creative Writing in North Carolina. Under the tutelage of professors like Margot Livesey, Joan Silber, Richard Russo, and Ehud Havazelet, Wroblewski learned much about crafting fiction—and yet, by his own admission, he still feels like a journeyman in the art of making stories work.

His smash-hit novel, *The Story of Edgar Sawtelle*, has seen the kind of success very few novels enjoy. Within weeks of its publication, in 2008 by HarperCollins, it had already hit the *New York Times* bestseller list, and a couple of months later, Wroblewski got the call from Oprah Winfrey herself saying she'd like to use *Edgar* for her Book Club.

Reminding us that good writing is always about the heart of a story and asking enough questions to get at a central problem characters face, David Wroblewski warmly shares his thoughts on crafting fiction, staying with your story, and getting lost in the love of the work.

*You worked as a software engineer before publishing **The Story of Edgar Sawtelle**. How has your previous job affected your approach to writing a novel?*

Well, the one word answer is *profoundly*. But the longer answer has to do with how writing software is like writing fiction, particularly writing novels. The kind of software I liked to make and gravitated towards is called exploratory programming. It involved asking, *could a program accomplish such and such?* We don't want to commit resources until we know we can do it. Somebody has to build a flimsy prototype that can fall apart just to prove that it can be done. That kind of programming is highly experimental. It involves starting out not knowing exactly what the problem is that you're trying to solve. It ends up being a search for a language in which the statement of the solution is beautiful. It's not a dry mathematical exercise, but very much more an aesthetic exercise. That is, you start out not knowing what you're after. By exploring many possibilities, playing with language, rearranging the parts, and so on, you come to understand both what the essential problem actually is, and what a good solution ought to be.

This can happen in writing as well. Software, for me, has largely been exploration in language. You do drafts, you get reviewed—very much like a workshop—you end up thinking about design. You learn how to hold these large complex structures in your mind, which is a skill you need while writing a novel. The list of craft correlations between making software and making fiction is so long that I always run out of time before I get to the end of the list. Most everything I learned about craftsmanship, I learned by making software. It transposes perfectly into writing.

Did you know you always wanted to pursue writing?

From the time I was eight or nine years old, I thought I was going to be an actor. I grew up in central Wisconsin—very rural, not much art of any kind easily available. But there was television, and movies, so I developed an interest in acting. That's where I always thought I was going to go. I did do a little writing in high school. I entered a state-wide competition and ended up winning a sort of grand prize for a short story I wrote, but that was a lark on my part, and I did it entirely to get out of school for one day. We were excused for a day to attend the art fair. All the award winners were posted. I completed my short story over a couple of nights on my mother's typewriter. During the ceremony, I wasn't paying attention. My best friend was sitting next to me, and he said, "They just called your name." My friend was a fantastic liar, so I didn't believe him. But then they called my name again. Still, I always thought I would be an actor, except for that one foray into writing. But then I did summer acting between high school and college and discovered that I didn't enjoy any aspect of the theatre except sitting in the audience. I switched my major from theatre to Computer Science and ended up getting that degree. Whatever the artistic impulse is in a person, it tends to manifest as making things or performing. For me, the only model I had was performing, so it took me a little while to sort that out.

What inspired you to begin crafting a novel?

Ten years out of college, I discovered that I had more time to pursue creative avenues other than software design. I published a paper on how software designers need to explore other creative arts. So, I had written some short stories that weren't very good; I realized that all of my short stories really wanted to be novels. That's when I went into the Warren Wilson Program because I really didn't understand novels. Why would you tell a story that is hundreds of pages long?

It's really an absurd form of telling a story. This happens to me a lot: I feel as though I intuitively understand something, but then I look at it closely and realize that I don't. I ask things like, why are there so many words in a novel? What is it about the novel that it has to be long?

How did you get Edgar from your initial pages to a contract offer for publication, and how long did the process take?

It depends on how you'd like to count it. My first words on *Edgar Sawtelle* were in 1993, and it was published in 2008. After I got out of the Warren Wilson program, I had about a third of a first draft. I wasn't in a big rush to publish anything, so I gave myself two kinds of permission. First, the book could be as long as it needed to be. Second, I could take as long as I needed to write it. That is, no superimposed word limit or timeline. As a novice, I had little chance of controlling those things anyway. I was working full time, and I would write at night. I completed a lot of drafts. Then at some point I'd had it, and I said, "I'm not going to touch this thing again until somebody says they want to publish it." I had gone through eight drafts; if I kept going, I was going to end up hating it by revising it to death. It's totally possible to revise a book past where you had it right. Over the course of a year or two, I found an agent who was willing to represent, and she eventually found a publisher. One footnote on all of this is that I called a few of my professors and said, "I feel like I could be working on this for the rest of my life. How do you ever know when to finish?" The answer I got was, "When you start editing it in a circle, and you've taken it as far as you can take it. Then you need an editor to step in from there."

Edgar has received praise for your intertwining of Shakespeare's Hamlet.

*However, you've stated that Edgar's journey more closely resembles Rudyard Kipling's **The Jungle Book**. Could you comment on the joys and difficulties of incorporating themes from past literary works?*

I think that *Edgar* has an equal allegiance to Shakespearean tragedy and *The Jungle Book*. I tried to keep the connections in the background, and whenever one or the other of those stories presented parallels, I would try to weave it in. It was great fun. I loved doing that. I think all stories draw on other stories. Sometimes it's more evident than other times, and that's fine, and sometimes it's very explicit. In *Edgar*'s case, it's in between. There's no reason that you would see any parallels to *Hamlet* until 40% into the book. My only frustration is that reviewers spoiled that surprise for readers. But Mowgli is introduced very explicitly in the book. For me, the allusions give it depth and make it interesting. These works have had great resonance for me in my life. In a way, it's homage to the stories that I love.

Do you write or read differently based on the acclaim Edgar has received?

I write differently because I have the experience of crafting a novel. You can begin to see how nothing is for free, and I am very aware of that whenever I read now. The little reviser in me is constantly saying, *Yeah, but what if you went into this?* It's rare now that I don't pick up a novel and experience it at some level as a question of design. But that would have been true even if *Edgar* had not been published; it's just the result of having written a novel, and therefore understanding just how many tradeoffs are involved. The hardest thing for me as a writer, reading, is to not jump into analysis too early and wonder what's wrong with the book as a whole. Those kinds of questions have to be put on hold.

How do you quell those critical voices and the pleas to analyze and judge your own work? How do you handle this?

I don't handle it too well, honestly. I'm always grateful when I get a stretch of an hour when the questions cease, and I feel lucky to enjoy writing like that. I feel *very* lucky when I have a day like that. I just sweat it out and remind myself that every writer goes through it. If you know of a strategy, I'd love to hear about it. You know, one of the things that I learned in the software world a long time ago is that you know you're doing the right thing if you get lost in the work. You look up at the clock and you say, *Oh, I can't believe it's five in the afternoon already*. It's that experience that you're shooting for, not any particular quality in your writing. For whatever reason, writers tend to be more critical. One of the reasons people enjoy programming so much is that the work is immersive; the program becomes a world in itself. Sometimes even a beautiful world, though invisible to anyone not directly and deeply engaged with the making. So, I know what it feels like when it's right. It's when I start to worry and judge that I don't have a solution. I generally try to do it by scoping down—work on a paragraph or a page. No matter how rotten of a day you're having, you can always get a paragraph.

Because so many writers have dreamed of this, I must ask about Oprah. Tell all. How did it happen, what did you feel, and what did that process do to your view of your work?

It was a very cool thing. It was a shock. I probably wouldn't tell you anything you'd be surprised by. It's certainly nothing you plan for, and I didn't see it coming. The book had been out for four months and had been on the *New York Times* bestseller list, and so the experience of being published already felt surreal. The day we talked on the phone, she said she liked the book, expressed her enthusiasm, and said she thought it would be a good selection for her list. It felt like a very discreet step away from reality. Usually, it's a slow drift. She is a genuine reader, she has so much passion for books, and her choices come out of her passion and tastes and nowhere else. I was thrilled. And honestly, I was really happy for my publisher. My publisher took a risk on a strange story, and I was glad that it paid off for him. It's not a no-brainer in the publishing industry. My editor worked incredibly hard for me. The sales staff at HarperCollins worked really hard for me. I was happy for myself, I was happy for the book, but I was also happy for the people who had championed the book. One of the things that you learn in making software is that, once the thing goes out into the world, you don't own it anymore. It goes on its own way. It has to either work or not, and you become auxiliary to the process. For much of the publication life of *Edgar*, I have been standing in the background, like an old uncle, wishing it well and sending postcards once in a while.

If you're willing to play along, could you suggest a few rules for writers that you believe are essential to follow?

Very, very little falls into an absolute category like that. For every rule, there's someone who has been very successful who has not followed that rule. The only one that seems somewhat universal is to write every day. But then, there are some writers who don't do that but still write very well. For myself, I try to write every day, and I try to do one other artistic work. I also do black and white photography, and I draw a lot from photography, because there are lessons to be learned in the process of making something else. When I'm feeling perfectionistic as a writer, because I'm also an amateur photographer, I can remind myself that something doesn't have to be perfect to be good.

What are some recent fiction titles you've appreciated or other recent books you would recommend that writers read?

Recently, I read *Crooked Letter, Crooked Letter* by Tom Franklin. The Warren Wilson MFA Program has a new book of essays by the faculty called *A Kite in the Wind*, I believe. All their books on writing are excellent, basically the lectures given in the program, written down and captured for posterity — wonderfully written essays. I just read *The Garden of Eden* by Ernest Hemingway, and it had one of the best descriptions of the actual experience of writing that I've ever come across. I think writers, particularly, will be interested in the latter half of that book, in watching the way that the main character handles his struggle to write.

John Robinson

I n a profoundly moving manner, John Robinson has personally inspired and propelled me to continue my journey as a writer. I first met John as an idealistic, wet-behind-the ears student-teacher. As a part of my degree in Secondary Education, I was paired up with the charismatic and passionate Mr. Robinson in Room 106 at Hamilton-Wenham Public High School in Massachusetts. Little did I know that my time spent at the school with the writer would not only inspire me as a teacher, but that it would activate and embolden my dreams as a writer.

Robinson's work has appeared in literary journals such as *The Sewanee Review, Ploughshares,* and a host of other literary magazines. He is also the author of two novels: *January's Dream* (Green Street Press, 1985) and *Legends of the Lost* (Northland Press, 1989). He is also the author of plays and essays while still being a passionate public high school English teacher for decades. Here, Robinson shares his wisdom, his encouragement, and his belief that rejections can become motivators for future work.

How have you diligently pursued your career as a writer while also teaching in the public schools?

During the course of my writing career, I have taught in fifteen different educational institutions—at universities, colleges, and secondary schools—in three different states. After graduation from college, I began teaching in the inner city of Chicago, and I experienced some of the most difficult times as a teacher and writer. I'd return home from a day of teaching feeling emotionally and physically spent. Back then, I was working on my first novel. It was very hard, but I felt if I didn't try every day, I would lose my ambition.

As the years went by, I learned to exploit the long summer vacations to create, using the September deadline for motivation. This is a huge advantage for writers who are in the teaching profession. During the hottest days of July, I would push myself. I wanted to be able to return for my fall classes knowing I had completed my story, novel, play, essay, and that it was being marketed as I toiled in the classroom. I was free then to devote myself—without regret—to my other passion: teaching literature and writing.

Where should fledgling or more experienced writers market their stories and essays?

The best places to go are the literary journals, sometimes called the "quarterlies," although there are very few magazines that actually publish four times a year. The great thing about the US literary journals is that most of them are financed by universities who are running MFA writing programs. Therefore, there is no consideration given to making money. The only thing that matters is quality, and there are hundreds of these journals in existence. It's important to note that there are several different tiers. Some are more esteemed than others, and a serious writer should know the difference. A web site called Bookfox (http://www.thejohnfox.com/) ranks them according to their *cachet* in the publishing world.

The quarterlies are good places to publish at *any* stage of a career. Editors and agents are constantly searching for new talent in them. The more elite journals pay cash for stories; the rest pay in contributors copies. But whether cash or copies, the importance of publishing your work in prestigious periodicals is critical. The journals are aesthetically magnificent with beautiful covers and gorgeous print. They are usually published in the quality trade paperback format, and therefore, can take a proud place on your shelf of published work.

It's good to recall that some of the greatest American writers—like Hemingway, Faulkner, and Flannery O'Connor—had their work published in literary journals. It's an honor to join their company. And the readership, though smaller in number than the national magazines, is far more serious. As a percentage, more subscribers are actually reading the periodical's contents than in the slicks, as the big circulation magazines are sometimes called.

Can you share some of the advice you give to young writers who are starting out on their journey to craft fiction?

Unless one is precocious, acquiring the gift of writing publishable fiction takes a long time, requiring patience and emotional stability, two virtues not easily accessible. But since all writers are at different stages of development, I think it's useful to divide a writing career into two parts.

The first part is the most difficult because the author has to learn on the job. As he struggles to create character and story, he makes mistakes; and if these mistakes are obvious to him, they can assist him in achieving his goal. But if these early miscues discourage him, this can lead to an early exit from his dream. The problem with the initial stage of a career is that there is less achievement, and therefore, less joy in creation. Breakthroughs are rare; awkwardness and frustration are common.

The hard part, then, is to keep going in the face of despair and defeat. But if a young writer is relentless in the pursuit of his dream, then small gains develop and grow into large victories, thus leading to the second part: seeing writing finally getting published. The most important exercise during this first phase is the act of self-congratulation. A neophyte writer needs to encourage and reward himself for the smallest of achievements.

The second part is easier than the first, but as a writer gets published and praised, the demands he makes on himself to get better, or to maintain the high quality he has already attained, grow. Now that the writer has cultivated his gift for language, he can fully partake in the joys of composition. It's what keeps him going. He is creating sentences, paragraphs, and pages of prose of which he once believed, in his darkest hours, he was incapable. But no more. Now he can immerse himself in his native language, enjoying both the initial writing, and later, the luxurious process of revision. I believe any writer who doesn't like to participate in the latter is not a real writer. It's in that final act of rethinking where the heights he has been seeking all along are finally scaled. Who would want to miss that journey?

I love the English language. I love writing it, reading it, and hearing it. All writers feel the same way.

How do you deal with the inevitable emotional roller coaster along the writer's journey? Have you found ways to create stability within a life of creativity? If so, can you share what you have learned?

Back in the early 1970's, I lived and wrote in Edinburgh, Scotland (and later Ibiza, Spain). I struggled with my novel at a large dining room table in a cold, second-story flat. I knew no writers, editors, or agents, and from the looks of what was emerging from my Olivetti electric typewriter, it seemed I never would. After a day's struggle, making feeble progress on my story, I wandered the medieval streets of Edinburgh reciting passages from great literature I'd memorized. The passages inspired me. They were the primary reason I wanted to become a writer. They were all I had on some of those dark nights. But they were enough. Somehow, some way, I said to myself, *I will write passages that someone will want to read and even one day want to publish.*

I come back, then, to the love of language: the beauty of the arrangement of words on a page. When lost, the best strategy to find your way is to return to the writing that "first gained access to your heart," as Albert Camus once wrote.

During that first year living abroad, I lived on little money and on little success. While all my friends were living back in the States advancing their careers and starting families, I was (I sometimes thought to myself) in Europe foolishly trying to write a novel.

But then one day, on a trip to the public library, I discovered Ernest Hemingway's *A Moveable Feast*. It saved my life. I'll never forget its final line: "But this is how Paris was in the early days when we were very poor and very happy." It perfectly summed up the entire experience of reading his memoir and of my real life as a struggling writer in Edinburgh.

Since you have written over the years in many genres, do you have a favorite?

I began, both as a reader and writer, as a novel snob. When I began writing fiction, I did not begin, as most logically do, with the short story. I never read short stories, only novels. Therefore, my first two fiction publications were both novels. I do not recommend this approach to anyone.

A quarter of a century ago, I fell in love with the short story. Many literary critics believe Americans are the best in the world in this genre, and yet most Americans who read fiction read novels. I began to enjoy reading the modern and contemporary masters of the form. I taught an undergraduate course in the short story, and that only intensified my passion. It was only a matter of time before I wanted to write short fiction.

If I could write in only one form to the end of my writing days, it would be the short story.

Can you share five of the books that might make your top ten list of all-time favorites?

1. *Julian* by Gore Vidal
2. *A Moveable Feast* by Ernest Hemingway
3. *The Collected Stories of Ernest Hemingway*
4. *Swan's Way* by Marcel Proust
5. *The Rabbit Tetralogy* by John Updike

Can you share a particularly difficult rejection story and how you overcame the emotion of that experience?

I like to answer this question in another way. The reasons for rejection are so varied —and sometimes flippant—that a writer should not be overly dejected when he receives a notice that someone has "passed" on his submission. Of course no one likes to be rejected, and it sometimes can be heartbreaking. But it's important to keep the rejection in perspective, especially if the author believes (as well as others whose opinion he trusts) his work is worthy of publication. And sometimes, the editor is correct and has convinced the author of the authenticity of his conviction. This understanding allows the author to jettison the project and begin to work on something that is more worthy of his time and effort.

Rejections, however, can also be inspirational. I remember

getting my first response from an editor that wasn't a form rejection. Instead, it was a personal letter extolling the virtues of what I had created while articulating the reasons for rejection. I was overjoyed. Later, another editor suggested revisions that would make my work publishable.

I graduated from these "passes" to encouragement to send more of my work. I slowly began to see my past shortcomings as a writer and how I had progressed since then.

The best procedure is to have multiple submissions of any single work. That way, if you get rejected, you know this is only one opinion.

What have been some of the rewards of choosing a writing career?

There have been so many. Beyond the obvious joy of seeing your work in print or your novels on the shelves of bookstores or libraries, there are the people you meet.

I have corresponded with and met many incredible writers, editors, agents, and readers. I have been able to assist talented writers as an instructor and colleague. I have formed lifetime friendships that are extremely valuable to me. These are things I never imagined.

Charles Baxter

As a deeply revered creator of literary fiction, Charles Baxter has been crafting powerful and revealing characters in literary fiction for more than thirty years. In 2000, his novel, *The Feast of Love* (Vintage), was honored with a National Book Award nomination. Baxter's long and varied publishing history is the product of a writer who thinks deeply about characters, creation, and craft.

Aside from his major novels, including his most recent, *The Soul Thief* (Vintage, 2008), Baxter has written widely in other forms. Originally getting his start with poetry, he initially thought his life would be dedicated to that form. However, after trying his hand at fiction, he began to see that the attributes of poetry could be applied there as well. Composing three novels over the course of his early years as a fledgling writer, Baxter often wondered if writing and publishing would ever become a part of his life. While none of those novels were ever published, a collection of short stories, *Harmony of the World* (Vintage, 1997), did garner a contract and was the first in a series of books that continue to acquire an ever-growing following and critical acclaim. He has also crafted two books on writing fiction, entitled *Burning Down the House* (Graywolf Press, 2008) and *The Art of Subtext* (Graywolf Press, 2007).

Here, Baxter's responses are often invitations towards discussion of craft and motivations behind creating art. At once an intellectually riveting responder, Baxter is deeply committed to the craft of literary fiction and in allowing the story to speak for itself.

You once wrote that, "We are here to serve the stories, not the other way around." Can you elaborate on the literary perception behind this idea and its implications for writers?

It's the art that's important; nobody really cares *who* writes these books. Writers should try to be selfless, but no one feels that selflessness starting out. When you're young, you want to make a name for yourself and establish your right to be on the planet. You want to be famous. What really matters, though, is putting yourself in the service of the work.

Fiction is often written out of a productive unhappiness. If you're happy all the time, why should you have any recourse to art? Every writer should feel, at least from time to time, as if he or she is an exile from happiness. I'm not the first to say that exile is a pretty good place to write from. Why should people who are perfectly happy have any desire to make art?

You wrote three novels before you began crafting short stories and then published your first collection. During the course of writing those novels, did you ever think about throwing in the towel?

I thought about it all the time. But I had this almost messianic idea that I had been put on the planet to write. So when no publisher wanted those novels, I suffered the despair that all young writers must go through. I spent months and years being rejected, and of course it was hard. I channeled those despairs into a short story, "Harmony of the World." That was a lesson for me. You can always put your demons to use if you try.

*A young writer comes to you and says, "I want to be a great novelist."
What's your reaction?*

I'd say, "Great—good luck. Be ready to suffer." It's not an
easy path, but in my own life, I was lucky: there were some
people at crucial points who encouraged me, and an almost
equal number of people who were terribly discouraging. The
angels balanced out the demons. Stubbornness saved me. It's
the stubbornness that makes it happen.

*How do you feel before you write, while you're writing, and after
you write?*

When I first started writing stories in my twenties, I would
approach my writing with excitement and a trace of nervous-
ness. I was excited about doing something worthwhile, yet
anxious about my ability to do anything of value. When writers
suffer from writer's block, it's usually because their insecurity
has gotten the upper hand over their writing.

When I got older, calculation became more a part of my
process. Before sitting down to write a story, I would daydream
about it, get to know the people. Patience is a great friend to
writers. You need to remind yourself that although you *don't*
have all the time in the world, the story will emerge if you take
your time with it, if you exercise patience, if you cultivate a
condition of watchful waiting.

When I write now in my sixties, I am entering a house that
I know pretty well.

*Your own work is characterized by people who follow tangents in their own
lives, and as a writer, you hold the camera on them as they go through
their series of confusing choices. How has this tendency developed in your
work, and how does it relate to the way you view the craft of fiction?*

I've never been sure, when writing stories or novels, how to proceed. I'll write pages—or I did, when I was writing on a typewriter—and then it would all go into the wastebasket. If there's a tangent that interests me, I'll follow it for as long as I can to see if it will be useful. I'm actually more interested in messiness than I am in a perfectly formed story. There can be an artfulness in a particular kind of messiness. I'd rather see the story go its own way as long as there's a central emotional anchor. That's what matters—the emotional logic of the story.

Of your own work, which book, story, or character would you say you love most? Why?

Chloé, a character in *The Feast of Love*. I didn't know where she came from—still don't—but I liked the energy of her character, and I liked her courage. I thought she would be a minor comic figure in the plot, but she had other ideas about her place in that story.

*You have written two books offering thoughts, theories, and guidance on writing fiction (**Burning Down the House** and **The Art of Subtext**). What books on craft and/or writing fiction would you recommend every writer have on her shelf?*

E. M. Forster's *Aspects of the Novel* has some useful observations about characterization; and David Jauss's *Alone with All That Could Happen,* a recent book, is very good about all the conventional wisdoms on certain matters of craft.

You've spoken about fatherhood and wondered if there was some instruction manual new parents should be given. As a writer, have you ever felt this way?

No, not really. If written literature is truly an art, then there can't be an instruction manual because no art is entirely rule-governed. Only beginners want the rules. Either there are no rules at all, or there are so many that you can't put them all into a book. You think you know what a novel is, and then something or somebody comes along to upset all your ideas. That's how art works. Of course, you have to know how to write sentences, and you need to have some ideas about how to create characters and set up a scene, but after that, the whole picture gets quite opaque.

How do you think new writers are best grown and developed?

I really don't know. They're good observers; they read; they don't mind solitude; they remember what people said and did; they're interested in ideas; they try to notice everything; they always feel slightly outside, looking in.

Toni Morrison has written that her stories must always have an impact on the "village" to mean something. Would you say your own work needs to have some certain impact, in your mind or in the minds of your critics or readers, to mean something?

Depends on what you mean, or she means, by "the village." I can imagine a story or a novel that somehow comes into its own years after it was written. "The village," whatever that was, in such a case didn't consist of a novel's contemporary readers but of readers decades in the future. Also, from a theoretical standpoint, a story can "mean" perfectly well without having a big boatload of audience members. I'm skeptical of the stance that says a book needs to be written to, or at, its audience. There can be bad consequences to that kind of thinking.

Many writers confess that they struggle most with middles. They open their novels, stories or nonfiction books with promise, but sweat out the middle pages in fear and self-loathing. While your work is not characterized by linear plotting, how would you say you make it through the metaphorical middle of one of your own books?

I keep asking the usual questions: What do these characters want? What are they afraid of? What's at stake in this story? Who's going to be hurt? How can I tempt them into taking interesting actions that will send the material forward?

A young writer comes to you with a worn leather satchel holding five manuscripts, pages all worn and some yellowing, sharing that no agent has taken her on. All the small publishers have turned her down. She's ready to quit. If she held your gaze with her own tired eyes and said, "Mr. Baxter... Charlie—can I call you Charlie?—what should I do?" how would you reply?

The easy and incorrect answer to this question is to say, "You must persist, no matter what." But clearly that response is sometimes wrong. Some would-be writers have no talent, and their work is shapeless and vacuous and poorly written and tedious. It's quite possible that the work has no value. These ideas must be entertained. I never know what to say when young writers ask me a question like that. I'm not the voice of history. Of course writers want to be encouraged, but if you encourage someone with no talent, you may be wrecking his life. There's much other work that needs doing in the world. As Donald Barthelme once said, "There are always paths, if you can find them; there is always something to do."

Forgive me this question, but you've spoken and written eloquently

153

about love: grasping for it, fumbling over it, using it as a drive. What would you say is the relationship between a writer and love?

No, forgive *me*. Whatever the relationship might be, it cannot be formulated in a few sentences.

Do you have any opinions on the trends in publishing lately — the rise in e-books, the marketing aspects, web sites, authors needing to push sales, or any other aspects?

No, I'm not a prophet, and I can't forecast any trends. It's all quite dizzying. I just try to stick to what I know I can do.

A lot has been said regarding literary fiction, its death or endangerment. What do you see as the state of literary fiction, and what would you say qualifies?

You never know. Clearly the middle-class infatuation with literary fiction is over; it collapsed decades ago. There's still a remnant, however, and the recent dust-ups over Jonathan Franzen's *Freedom* show that there may be quite a few readers out there for a certain kind of fiction. But, as I said, the audience may be a remnant, and literary fiction may be a remnant art. Look, I started writing my books with a pen and paper and a typewriter. I graduated to a word processor and then to a computer. Technologies advance, and they bring with them different kinds of storytelling. Milan Kundera has claimed recently that we are in an era of post-art. Art, he might say, can no longer compete with other distractions. What we have instead is mass-produced kitsch. I don't know. Thinking too much about these big questions can lead to paralysis. If you like stories, then you read stories, and, in some cases, try to write them. What the world does with your work is not really up to you anyway.

Ann Hood

A writer who deals openly with grief—both her own and that of her characters—Ann Hood became a full-fledged author when airline TWA employees went on strike and flight attendants found themselves replaced. Since then, Hood has written scores of essays, magazine features, novels, and nonfiction. Her work has been in the pages of *The New York Times*, *Ploughshares*, *The Paris Review*, *Good Housekeeping*, *Tin House*, and other magazines and literary journals. Her book credits include, among others, the novels *Somewhere Off the Coast of Maine* (Bantam 1987), *Places to Stay the Night* (Doubleday 1993), *The Knitting Circle* (W.W. Norton 2008), *The Red Thread* (W.W. Norton, 2011) and the nonfiction books, *Creating Character Emotions* (Story Press, 1998), *Do Not Go Gentle: My Search for Miracles in a Cynical Time* (Picador 1999), *Comfort: My Journey through Grief* (W.W. Norton 2008). Here, she shares about her journey with candor and clarity.

What makes your heart beat fast as a writer?

When I look up from my computer and hours have passed without me even realizing it. The light has shifted. The house's sounds are different. And I realize I've been in that magical zone with just me and the writing.

You've written about very difficult events in your life. How does writing affect and interact with the pain about which you write?

It never gets easier to write about grief. I just wrote an essay for Salon, and for two days afterward, I could do nothing but hide under a blanket with the Food Channel on TV. But it's important to do it. Literature is made up of the grief and heartache of writers. The hope is that by articulating it, others will be able to say, *Yes, that's me...*

What kinds of writing support do you need or greatly appreciate as you work?

I basically like to be left alone. Again, I like to exist in that zone of just me and words.

Can you share one of your most painful rejections and one of your most meaningful acceptances?

I always have to point to the day I got word that my first novel, *Somewhere Off the Coast of Maine,* as my most meaningful acceptance. I was working as a TWA flight attendant, and here I got my first novel accepted for a large (in those days) sum of money. It changed my life.

I don't take rejections badly. I believe that good writing always finds a home. The times when someone led me to believe something would be accepted and then reneged on that promise were disappointing, but certainly not devastating.

If a young novelist or memoirist or poet tapped you on the shoulder right now and said he couldn't take the rejection and uncertainty of writing anymore, what would you say in reply?

Find a different career.

What disciplines help you stay focused and creative as a writer?

Reading everything I can get my hands on. Knitting. Cooking. Walking.

Can you share the story of your first publication (book, article, or otherwise) and what that experience was like—any emotions, contemplations, or lessons associated with it?

Somewhere Off the Coast of Maine was one of the two launch books of a series called Bantam New Fiction, which began in 1987. So it was published with great fanfare—lavish parties, book signings at big stores on 5th Avenue, a spot on *Good Morning America*. It was a dizzying and dazzling experience.

Can you share a list of your favorite works or works that inspire you deeply?

The Great Gatsby, by F. Scott Fitzgerald
My Antonia, by Willa Cather
The stories of John Cheever, Raymond Carver, and Anton Chekov
Dinner at the Homesick Restaurant, by Anne Tyler

What most irks you and delights you about the enterprise of getting a book published in today's business?

I find the experience delightful, for the most part. I have been blessed with a talented, smart, enthusiastic editor and a team of dedicated creative people who work so hard for my books. With rare exceptions, I have found this to be true for my whole career. New writers invite disappointment, I think, by sending out work that isn't ready for publication. But I do believe what I said above: good writing gets published.

John Dufresne

A veritable fount of wisdom for the seeking writer, John Dufresne's fiction and nonfiction are breathtaking. As a master of creativity and possessing a never-ending supply of energy, Dufresne is also one of the most compassionate and inspiring writers you're likely to read. His volume, *The Lie That Tells a Truth* (W.W. Norton 2004), is one of the most original takes on the writing process that's been delivered. His fiction, including *Love Warps the Mind a Little* (W.W. Norton 1997), which was chosen as a *New York Times* Notable Book of the Year, has been hailed as inventive and authentic. Sharing his characteristic wit and compassion for the struggling writer, John Dufresne's responses provide both a pat on the back and a kick in the behind simultaneously, which is, in itself, a feat.

You have received much praise for your books on writing, including **The Lie That Tells a Truth** *and, most recently,* **Is Life Like This?** *What inspired you to craft these books, and how do you find the passion to encourage other writers with such wisdom and energy?*

I've been teaching fiction writing for over twenty years, so I think about stories all the time. Not only do I have to think about them, I have to figure out how best to explain my thoughts about writing to beginning writers. So I've been taking notes and shaping lectures and essays about the craft and then one day decided to put them all together. And then I thought I'd focus on the problems and opportunities of the novel specifically, and I had another book. I love reading stories and I want more great stories to read, so if I can help someone learn the craft and write me those stories, I'm thrilled.

Is there any person (or people) who helped you embrace your writing career? If so, how did they do it?

I had a teacher in high school, Brother Joseph Gerard, who was the first person that told me I could write and that I might be a good writer one day. That's all the encouragement I needed. I already wanted to be a writer, and I had just discovered that it was stories I wanted to write. At grad school, William Harrison and Jim Whitehead taught me everything I know. This was at the University of Arkansas. Harrison was a genius at plot. Whitehead insisted on passion and heart. Both were rigorous and tolerated no bullshit. There was no complacency allowed. So what if that last story was praised in workshop? Write another one—and not the same one.

What inspires you as a writer?

Telling stories about people who don't exist. When I get to know these people, I just want to know them better and I want to do justice to their lives, which are going to be full of strife. Telling the story and getting the words right—the language and the music of it. Nothing better than finding the miraculous adjective.

What, if anything, deflates you as a writer?

I suppose reading bad writing does. But you don't read it for long. Pedestrian writing is not the business I want to be in.

I want to be doing what Chekhov did—and I know I'll never get there, but it's worth trying. About the writing process, I never feel deflated. I may feel unsuccessful some days, but that's how it goes. Hair stylists, I'm sure, have good styling days and not so good. Even Ted Williams only succeeded a third of the time.

What are some common misconceptions about publishing that you think non-published writers often hold?

When I was an unpublished writer, I thought getting a book published would be impossible. The publishing world was a galaxy far, far away. I would encourage young writers not to think about the publishing business at all. Think about writing and about your stories. Just write, write, write until your fingers bleed and read everything you can get your hands on. They say it takes 10,000 hours of practice to get good at anything. Put in those hours and then worry about publishing.

Well, that might be ideal, but it's impractical and unrealistic. We want to see our darlings on the page; we want people to read our stories. I do believe that if you write something beautiful, compelling, and transcendent, you will get it published, but maybe not when and where you want it to be.

One misconception might be that a lot of money can be made. And it can, but that's not likely. If you get a $100,000 advance on your novel, and it takes you three years to write it, that's $33,000 a year and 15% of that goes to your agent and 25% of what's left to the government. Can you live well on what's left? Of course, maybe you can write really fast. I have a friend who quit his day job—lawyer—to write full time, and he is down to his last thousand dollars and is scrambling to get any kind of job he can. Sorry, overqualified.

In working with students, what do you find yourself frequently advising?

You have to read constantly and widely. And you have to write every day. No holidays. This is work. It's a job—a great job—but if you don't punch in, you don't get paid. You have to read the classics and the contemporaries. You have to read fiction and nonfiction and poetry. You're an apprentice, and you need to learn to use your tools. "Read, read, read. Read everything—trash, classics, good and bad, and see how they do it. Just like a carpenter who works as an apprentice and studies the masters. Read! You'll absorb it. Then write. If it's good, you'll know it. If it's not, throw it out the window." William Faulkner said that. And always be writing. I know I'm repeating myself. Write on the bus, write in your pajamas, write a letter to your mom, write a story, write a song, write a grocery list (and turn that into a poem) write, write, write until your fingers bleed. If you're a fiction writer, yes, you need a plot. Find out what one is and use it. Let the plot guide the writing of your story.

Do you adhere to any "writing rules" for yourself? If so, can you share some of them and how you first incorporated them into your work as a writer?

The first commandment of writing is, *Sit your ass in the chair*! And here are the other nine:

2. Thou Shalt Not Bore the Reader.
3. Remember to Keep Holy Your Writing Time.
4. Honor the Lives of Your Characters.
5. Thou Shalt Not Be Obscure.
6. Thou Shalt Show and Not Tell.

7. Thou Shalt Steal.

8. Thou Shalt Rewrite and Rewrite again. And again.

9. Thou Shalt Confront the Human Condition.

10. Be Sure That Every Death in a Story Means Something.

I try to live by those commandments, but sometimes I sin.

Can you share a particularly difficult rejection story and how you overcame the emotion of that experience?

The writing life is one of rejection. If you have a thin skin, do something else. Editors reject your work, and so do critics. There are two kinds of critics—the professional critic of whom Brendan Behan wrote, "Critics are like eunuchs in a harem; they know how it's done, they've seen it done every day, but they're unable to do it themselves." Hemingway called them "camp-following eunuchs." Every rejection stings. You soothe the pain by writing—and that's the only way. I don't have any terrible rejection stories. The narrator of my novel, *Love Warps the Mind a Little*, is a struggling writer who writes indignant responses to the venomous rejections he gets from editors. That's not a good idea. Don't waste your time. Don't respond to critics; it's unbecoming and pointless. There are editors and critics who respond positively to writers who write like they do and scold writers who have the audacity to take risks in their work.

Know that unseemly literary scores are settled in this ignoble public forum. Don't pay too much attention to them. You're not as good as they say you are; you're also not as bad. Criticism is inevitable and welcomed because without it, literary culture would collapse; but criticism, as Auden said, should be a casual conversation, not the thunder and lightning and vitriol that it too often becomes. Still, better a tempest of invective than glacial indifference. Look at what it was that irritated the critic or critical editor about your book and go there. That's where you were doing something new, something he could not understand, and that's the itch to scratch.

Can you share the story of your first publication (book, article, or otherwise) and what that experience was like—any emotions, contemplations, or lessons associated with it?

I had a few story publications, some in prestigious places, and I had enough stories to put a collection together. I read through a book on agents—maybe the Writer's Digest book, I can't remember. There were exactly three agents who were interested in seeing short stories. I sent each of them three stories and said I had nine more. One of them, Richard McDonough, wrote me back and asked to see the rest. He liked them and he's still my agent. He shopped the book around for a year at least, and it would get lots of praise and enthusiasm from an editor at a house, but then get rejected at the staff meeting. Finally Jill Bialosky at Norton took it and got her colleagues to agree. She's still my editor. When I got the call from Dick that Norton had taken the book, I was standing in my kitchen in Augusta, Georgia, and I was so ecstatic I could not speak. I just kept walking in circles. He told me the advance was small, and I said, "I would have paid them." He said, "We won't tell them that."

Bill Roorbach

Writing is a deep passion for Bill Roorbach, evident by the scope of what he has been able to accomplish. His writing has appeared in publications as various as *Harper's, Newsday, Ecotone, The American Literary Review,* and *The Atlantic Monthly.* His books include collections of short stories (*Big Bend,* University of Georgia Press 2001), novels (including *The Smallest Color,* Counterpoint 2001), memoirs (including *Summers with Juliet,* Ohio State University Press 2000), and even a volume on craft (*Writing Life Stories,* Writer's Digest Books 2000). Roorbach has taught Creative Writing at The University of Maine, Ohio State University, and Holy Cross. Currently, he writes full time in every conceivable genre he can touch and does so with verve and wit.

What makes your heart beat fast as a writer?

Too much medicinal tincture of hashish, whoa! (Still recovering from a serious operation on my neck.)

You've written about your family in your work, and you often utilize humor to create poignant meanings. How has family inspired you to write, or how have they hindered your journey as a writer?

My wife has often been a character in my nonfiction, and now my daughter, too, born in 2000. One inspiration is that I need to make money to keep us all fed! Kids especially take time, but that journey has put my writing career in perspective—it all seems easy after parenting.

Can you share one of your most painful rejections and one of your most meaningful acceptances?

I think no rejection has been worse than Carla in high school. As for writing, I just don't think of it the way I used to. Rejection just seems part of the game these days after so many and after some acceptances. I guess the worst of the rejections have to be early on: My first novel, *The Smallest Color*, was turned down dozens of times before Counterpoint took it. And that acceptance was a real party, though it was my fourth book.

Which books inspire your own craft?

Anything really good across a very wide spectrum. I really don't know where to start. Early on, I couldn't read while writing because I would turn into that writer. Now my own voice is pretty firm, so not even a hardcore stylist like Faulkner gets in my head, stertorous and miscegenation and the clinking of cooling engine blocks and all that.

What kinds of writing support do you need or greatly appreciate as you work?

Time is the great blessing. And a place to work. I love my studio. And I love that it's only a hundred yards from home. My daughter used to come in and pretend to write alongside me at my desk. Now she really does write, hours at a time.

If a young novelist or memoirist or poet tapped you on the shoulder right now and said he couldn't take the rejection and uncertainty of writing anymore, and that he sought you to help him find the chutzpah to keep going, what would you say in reply?

I would say try to quit. If you can, wonderful. If you can't quit, then all you can do is keep going. And try to find your pleasure in the making, because that's the only pleasure you're going to get.

You've got a hilarious and meaningful blog on writers and writing that you run with David Gessner (billanddavescocktailhour.com). How has blogging influenced your writing, and what are your thoughts and feelings about your work on the blog?

We write a lot for that thing. We're learning to write short. And it's really great to have an instant audience, instant reaction. It's almost like playing music. You have a sense of the audience, even if they're just booing.

Can you share the story of your first publication (book, article, or otherwise) and what that experience was like—any emotions, contemplations, or lessons associated with it?

My first real publication was "Into Woods," a short memoir about wood shop and my father that ran in Harper's Magazine. I was shocked when my father bought the magazine and called to tell me he was going to read my piece: I hadn't yet been confronted by my characters. He called back crying. I tell the story in detail in my book of instruction, *Writing Life Stories,* and the essay is at the back of that book. You can probably find it online as well.

Lindsey Collen

The very definition of an activist-writer, Lindsey Collen achieved international renown and critical claim for her work when she wrote her novel, *The Rape of Sita* (Feminist Press 1993), for which she won the Commonwealth Writer's Prize for Africa in 1994. The book also got her long listed for the prestigious Orange Prize in 1996. Collen is also the author of the novels *There is a Tide* (Ledikasyon pu Travayer 1990), *Getting Rid of It* (Granta Books, 2007), *Mutiny* (Bloomsbury, 2001), and *Boy* (Bloomsbury 2004). Collen's most recent novel is *The Malaria Man & Her Neighbours*. Her work is characterized by lucid language, rich storytelling, and a commitment to ideals of social justice, women's rights, and advocating for the voiceless and mischaracterized. Her work deals boldly with themes of violence and how society both endangers and normalizes violence against women and those who speak out. In this regard, Collen shares harrowing details of the threats she has faced from publishing her work and for her commitments as a writer. This interview highlights notions of creativity, purposes of why we write, and the very personal and yet also highly universal struggles and obstacles we must overcome in order to write truthfully—even if we're writing fiction.

Your work battles misogyny and patriarchy in powerful ways. What have been the struggles you've faced in this journey?

For the journey *as a writer*, telling stories should be a straightforward thing. But if, when you tell stories, you also perhaps expose and chronicle, define, and oppose things like misogyny and patriarchy, you can get hurled into unexpected struggles. I've faced only *one* such struggle, and it was a very hard one. It was when I was accused, at one and the same time, by a group of fundamentalists of being a blasphemer and by the State of being both a blasphemer and "an outrage against public and religious morality" under the Criminal Code.

This put me in an extremely precarious position. My life was certainly not worth much at that point. I was threatened by one lot with death and public rape, and the State, instead of protecting me, threatened me with seizing copies of my book, arresting me, and slapping criminal proceedings on me.

I was also psychologically somewhat febrile at the time because, as other novelists will perhaps bear witness, when you first publish a new novel, there is a vulnerability you feel for having exposed yourself. I do anyway. It's as if, at the launch, you stand naked before readers. In truth, you stand there. I suppose this feeling is born of that particular stage during the process of creating a novel, when I find myself in that particular state of mind that we are usually in *only when we are all alone at night*, during a dream. The daytime censors are down. And it is, like in a dream, a very private time. So, in a novel, there remains something of that same rawness that exists in our dream narratives. The only difference is that, as you write a novel, even when in this weird state of mind, you can somehow give direction, form, and a certain humor to the dream process as it unfurls otherwise unconsciously. Just as it does in a dream, it weaves in things from your past life, recent and long ago, with events you've never experienced but have only heard about, together with other things that are clearly and completely made up, but with that same wild and untamed symbolism that dreams have. Anyway, it was during this moment of feeling quite exposed and vulnerable, at the very time of putting my novel out in public, that I was attacked.

So, that is what I felt like at the publication of *The Rape of Sita*, the novel that caused me to be attacked so violently. This was in 1994.

I was attacked only partly *because* of writing the novel *The Rape of Sita*, and in particular because of its title, which was what people objected to. But it happened also *because* I am a political activist in a left political party, incidentally called *Lalit* (meaning *struggle* in Mauritian Kreol and *beautiful* in Hindi), which is, at the very least, a persistent thorn in the side of the powers-that-be. At best, it is a constant reminder to everyone of the possibility that Mauritian society could, with a little courage from us oppressed together with all thinking people, be a much better place to live in for everyone. Most people at the time firmly believed I was attacked only because I was one of the opponents of the politicians in power, though this obviously was not sufficient cause.

Curiously, and yet also naturally, the struggle against the death threats and threats of prison was made dignified for me and relatively easy to face up to precisely because I was an active member not only of a fantastic political party, but also of a vibrant women's organization. My novel was, in addition, published by a workers' education organization. We had sold 150 prepaid vouchers before it came out so as to fund the novel's printing costs (which were consequently already sold before the book got attacked and banned). This pre-release selling turned out to be one of the ways we would fight against the repression with which I was so violently threatened. My friends and colleagues went around distributing the novel in brown paper wrappers to people who had already paid for it. We could get around the law this way because all it said was that it was illegal to "expose the book for sale." This distribution then, in turn, permitted people to read the novel and allowed them to defend it. It is not always easy for everyone to defend a banned book when they can't read it.

So, I found myself supported very well indeed by networks of people with whom I already had shared programmatic ideas and common socio-political work. I never in my wildest dreams thought these networks might save my life! How blind of me.

In the village I lived in, I was saved in a similar way. I was a collector for a health co-operative that grouped some 500 families, who paid monthly dues, for medical care provided by the association. The doctor of the co-op was Ram Seegobin, my partner, and I was one of twelve people who each had one-twelfth of the village to collect dues from. So once a month, I had paid a visit to the homes of some forty families in the village, sat in their kitchens as they prepared the evening meal, or took their newest baby into my arms and chatted. This went on for over a decade. I became a *zanfan lakaz*, or child of the hearth, to all these families and to their neighbors. And since my husband looked after the health of half the families in the village, when there were medical emergencies, I found myself welcomed into peoples' homes, as Ram's partner, at times when people hid nothing from outside eyes. I was a privileged visitor. And this, as well as bringing me deeper into village society than any writer could hope to be brought, also made for very close emotional ties with people beyond our circle of friends. And they could then defend me when I was under attack.

Perhaps equally importantly on a nationwide scale, I had been in the forefront of the organization of the biggest workers' movement—a general strike movement—in August 1979, that went on in September, 1980, challenging the very State. So, I am known personally in the houses of laborers, sugar factory workers, and other poor people all over the country from those times of bringing and taking news and decisions from the union headquarters to the sugar fields. It was thus not so easy to paint me as a witch, less still a foreign witch.

All this is to say that my life was saved by the very political engagement that contributed towards bringing down the threats upon me in the first place!

My friends, colleagues, and comrades were also able to galvanize an unexpected amount of support from writers and other artists in Mauritius. I was unconditionally and bravely supported by almost every single writer in the country, something I would not have dreamed of hoping for. Letters of support poured in from abroad as well, and they did not come all by themselves. People needed to be informed, and this demanded very dedicated, highly skilled political work. There was also a stroke of luck: the Commonwealth Writers' Prize for the Africa Section was awarded to *The Rape of Sita*, and it became very well known and was soon also out in British, German, Danish, and Dutch editions. The Pen "Writers in Prison" Committee in London, the Article XIX association, and the Index of Censorship all took up the threats against me.

But at the same time, we had to prepare a long-term strategy to get the book back on the shelves. The kind of strategic planning that was necessary would not have been possible had I been a writer sitting in isolation at a computer. But, because of my daily involvement in struggles, this one took its place amongst the others in my life. This time it was for free expression, and it was also for women's emancipation in a very direct way. Before the huge confrontations around the title of the book, the issue of rape had been swept under the carpet in Mauritius. Women were blamed for it. Women were considered to have sought it. People could claim that rape was "impossible." It was confused with consensual sex. Marital rape was not recognized as rape. If a young woman was raped, her family might get out a shotgun and force a marriage for her upon the perpetrator. This was something not too unusual.

So the struggle for the novel to get back on the shelves was also the struggle to get rape exposed for what it is: aggression. And it was a struggle that exposed the games played by groups of fundamentalists. They are relatively small groups, and their link to religion is fairly flimsy in that they merely find ways of *using* it. And although I was under attack from Hindu fundamentalists, when opposing them, we learned general lessons about the nature of all fundamentalists. In particular, we learned how they are a *political* current, and it is often one that breeds on genuine suffering but through very manipulative processes. When there are empires that seem impregnable and that are dominating local communities, and when there are neither political voices courageous enough to expose this evident truth nor farsighted enough to oppose this obvious adversary, then fundamentalist currents, hiding behind religious impunity, offer a "surrogate voice" against the mighty. And they play this out just as you or I might play a game of cheat, quite consciously and unabashedly using the most outrageous tactics. Amongst these tactics, you find attacking artists (who are often fairly isolated), attacking women (witch-hunting is still big), attacking foreigners (a bit of xenophobia can sometimes be whipped up), and maligning those seeking genuine change in society (spreading calumny that is hard to reply to). All this in the guise of defending against what is often genuine repression in society, and all this feeding on genuine suffering.

The struggle against the banning and the threats also taught me and a whole generation of us how important literature is or can be, and how important it can be considered by authorities to be. Although, in the case of *The Rape of Sita*, it was the title that was opposed, not the work itself. The contempt for the title of my novel also exposed a wealth of otherwise hidden assumptions that were rife in society: mainly, that rape must be the victim's crime.

Anyway, eventually we got the book out again. A very happy ending.

I'd also like to add something important at a personal, family level. The fundamentalists that attacked me (male, the lot of them) would, in articles published in the press, try to goad my brothers-in-law and husband into roles as controllers of an out-of-bounds woman in the family. But this only made them laugh, so I was lucky there. We were always, in Ram's family, rather sorry that my father-in-law was no longer alive by that time because he would have had a field day against the fundamentalists.

My father had an unusual take, too, when I told him: he said, quite calmly, that he thought it "unfair" of the State to come down on someone already under attack by fundamentalists.

But for me, the most difficult part was that I had written about rape, a most difficult subject emotionally. It had taken all the powers of self-examination and memory that I could muster to manage to write that novel. And then the attack on me, when it came, felt like something akin to a rape. Indeed, I was threatened with actual rape. It was as though the horror of rape that I had exposed in the novel was to be forced upon me as revenge for my having exposed it.

Growing up, were there any experiences that you see as formative to your journey as a writer? Or, in a broader scope, how do you see your childhood contributing to or hindering your work as a writer?

I think my childhood experiences, the structure of my experience, does contribute directly to my ending up a writer and to the kinds of things I write about, too. From when I was two years old until I was five, we lived in such a remote rural area that I did not really have a peer group. This was in South Africa, in the times of apartheid. This lack of a peer group when I was learning human language has, I think, created in me the capacity to be totally dedicated to something done collectively with other people and also to be watching from the outside as if alone. I think a writer can benefit from this ability to be right in something and yet also able to observe it from the kind of solitude in which one writes.

And then, of course, the love of language I developed at that very young age is also probably very important. I became, at that key period in my life, the only human being who could speak all three languages that were spoken in the four units around the two houses that were the outcrop we lived in then. The neighbors spoke no English but only Afrikaans, which my mother did not speak well at all; and although my father spoke it, he was out at work all day, so I picked it up and soon spoke it perfectly. And the household workers at the two homes, who looked after me and the neighbor's baby as well as the two houses and their little gardens, all spoke a third language. I think it was Tswana, and I soon spoke it fluently, too, as they knew neither English nor Afrikaans. My parents spoke only Xhosa of the African languages, not Tswana. So, not only did I hear three different languages and kinds of narratives, but I also became the translator who was called in to interpret for any other two people, literally, day in and day out. My mother would describe to me years later how I would be summoned to interpret, and how I would look at the speaker, concentrating like mad, listening to every word, and then there would be a silence while I absorbed the meaning of what the person had to say. Then I would generate the same idea in the other language for the listener. She said it was an utterly unique thing to watch, and that it made her realize how languages were not mirror images of each other. Speaking all three, she said, was clearly one thing, and that being able to translate from one to the next was another.

Also at this key period, my middle brother was born when I was two and a bit. My mom would obviously spend a lot of time with him; so my father then spent hours in the evenings reading to me, mainly from a big old-fashioned book with gold edgings full of fairly adult versions of Greek and Roman stories. That was what I insisted he read to me—no children's books. So stories became a way of life. When I was given a doll for my third birthday, I announced to my mother that she was called "Sibyl," to which she said, "Where on Earth did you ever hear that name?" Of course, from the stories of the woman prophesiers of Rome my dad read to me.

From that time, I was also probably somehow aware of "the State" in its bare bones, and this is something that is always in my writings: a kind of seeing of the State, and a love of collective life of people despite it, outside of its purview, in opposition to it. You see, my father was the lone magistrate, representing the judiciary and the civil status office. The neighbor was the lone policeman, representing law and order. People ran their lives for miles and miles of radius around, mainly oblivious to this colonial vestige of the repressive State. Yet, its presence was there—one of the worst States ever. And I could see the interrelated parts of the State so clearly: the judiciary, the police, the family; and as I grew up, it was easy to add in "religion," "the press," and the legislature. So to me, the State is not as reified nor as mystified as it might be for other people. Nor is it impregnable. Nor is it inevitable. Nor can it be ignored. I think I can see bureaucratic "facts" separately from peoples' collectively lived lives—a talent peasants used to have, but one that is not so common in this day and age anymore.

Let me just outline where I lived during my childhood so

that you can get an idea of the geographical and social changes I went through just by changes in geography. This, too, has perhaps given me a perspective that is unusually independent of any one place:

- Born while parents lived in Mqanduli, in the rural Transkei, as it was called, now part of the Eastern Cape of South Africa.
- When I was one year old, my father was transferred to the capital city, Pretoria, in the Rand area.
- At two years old, he was transferred to that outpost described above in the Northern Transvaal, called Bochom, and later spelt Bochem.
- At five years old, we moved to Cala, a fairly large village back in the Transkei in the Eastern Cape, where we lived for two years.
- At six, I spent six months until the end of the school year with my maternal grandparents in Mqanduli, a small village, because my father had been transferred to a large city, Pietermaritzburg in KwaZulu Natal, where the school systems were very different.
- From the ages of seven to eleven, we lived in a big city, Pietermaritzburg.
- Then, at eleven, my father was moved back to Qumbu in the Transkei. I stayed on with two different sets of friends for six months to complete primary school under this system. The second of these was in a family involved in a political campaign to "Stop the Prime Minister Verwoerd from coming into Pietermaritzburg," which I got involved in at age eleven.
- Then at twelve years old, I went to boarding school because in Qumbu there was no secondary school for children classified "white." This was in the city of East

London, a seaside city. Here, I had plenty of peer groups to make up for what I hadn't had when I was young, but then I was impervious to it.

- Before my schooling ended, my father had been transferred to work at Alexandra Township in Johannesburg. We took up residence there and I attended the University of Witwatersrand.

So, I lived in eight different places. This sure makes for understanding cultural relativity. But I think more than that it gave me a more varied "structure of feeling," in the sense in which Raymond Williams uses the term, than most people have. This opens my work to empathize with people from quite different walks of life. I also knew that my father, not some other magistrate, was being transferred to places where the State was having difficulty keeping "law and order" for the double reason that he was being punished for being an opponent of the Nationalist Party, and that he was being sent because the State could not manage to keep apartheid's order.

It left me with a feeling that my life was hurtling towards conflict, because it was, and so I seem to have been blessed with little fear of conflict. I was also aware that the places I spent many years in—Mqanduli, Cala, and Qumbu—were on the line where there was never quite a defeat of the African people by the colonizer, but where there was only a truce. I am left with a feeling, too, of being able to recognize fault lines in State domination, so I have a kind of built-in hope for change towards a better society. The feeling of living where until recently nomadic peoples, who had lived for maybe 50,000 to a 100,000 years in harmony and equality and without a State, were always there. So such times can come around again.

Living in so many places also meant that reading and writing were an important part of the consistency I maintained during an ever-changing life. It was part of myself.

My mother, throughout all this, shared with me—we were so close, she called me "sis," for as long as I can remember— her constant political criticism of not only apartheid but of class society and of colonialism. Being married to a civil servant in those days meant not only was he not allowed to do politics, but she, as his wife, was not allowed to either, and she hated this. I remember once my father made a comment, lightly, during a minor argument about how lucky she and her three kids were (they were his, too) that he didn't drink and beat her and them up every week (an allusion to his work as magistrate, no doubt). My mother later told me that that was the real definition of women's oppression: you had to feel lucky you weren't beaten up. "Isn't that just the bottom!" she said. She made such a point of this "lesson to a daughter" that I remember it clear as a bell even today. I must have been no older than eight years old at the time, maybe even younger.

My maternal grandparents, Scots from Aberdeen, book-keepers turned small shopkeepers living in Mqnduli, were also quite Bolshie. Once when I was about six, my granny was staying with me and asked if I knew what the most sell-out ruling class in the world was. How could I know such a thing? "The Scots," she said.

On a similar note, my paternal grandmother was a Scot, married to my grandfather, a Cockney, and they worked as baker and patissiere together in Umtata. During arguments, she would threaten him with the Battle of Bannockburn. It is the name of a village in Scotland where some river was reputed to have run red with the blood of English soldiers for a week after some Scots slaughtered them.

What is the most enjoyable part of the writing process for you?

What I like most is also what is most daunting, most terrifying, and it feels like a total risk. Like sky diving. I never think I'll be able to do it again. I *always* think I'll never be able to do it again.

It is when I feel that my rough notes in second-hand ledgers are now vast enough, that ideas have begun to take form enough around structures, characters, narratives, that I am ready to go and isolate myself for the next three weeks by the sea with a computer and sit from dawn to dusk, drafting the whole novel right through. This is an exhilarating experience. Utterly thrilling. Totally absorbing. The very highest of worldly pleasures. The feeling of both creating a narrative and preparing a present, a gift. It is like a performing art for those three weeks. And being kept a total secret until it's finished adds to its complete delight.

Once you begin a project, how do you discipline yourself to follow it through?

I have a serious problem when I'm preparing notes for a new novel. I have too many novels jostling around in my mind at the same time, trying to get out. Some seven, usually, and I have one helluva time trying to exclude six from my mind and from my notes. That's the first problem. Then I eventually build up enough notes.

*For your novel, **The Rape of Sita**, can you share your journey from start to finish? How did you complete the book, and how did the process of publication happen for you?*

I wrote the first draft of *The Rape of Sita* in three weeks straight, literally in a fever of writing. Then over the next two years, I honed it. I would work every morning for a couple of hours before doing other things, refining some aspects of the draft, developing others. The biggest change was, in fact, when

I cut out about a third of the story. There was a whole element of the narrative that dealt with the effect on Sita *afterwards*, of both the rape itself and then losing all memory of it, and I had to decide either to develop it more deeply or to cut it. I decided to cut it because it slowed the already complicated narrative down, convincing myself it would need another whole novel to do it justice. (But I have never come back to that—well, not yet anyway.) Cutting things is always problematic because I get very attached to some of them. And then, even though I can see it doesn't sit very well in the novel, I can't easily throw it away. So, the trick I use is to convince myself I'll use the material later, though oftentimes, I don't need to.

The process of publication was very integrated. I submitted the manuscript to the workers' education publishers who had already published my first novel, *There is a Tide*, and they decided to publish it. They are also a printer, so together we organized the same prepaid voucher system as for the first novel. We sold between 100 and 150 vouchers, which covered the big layout on paper for the printing, and we organized a good launch party. I remember it was at the house of a friend, also in *Lalit*, who is a classical pianist recently converted to jazz, and she played beautiful music at the launch. There were two launch speeches, one by Jeanne Gerval Arrouf and the other by Shakuntala Hawoldar, who both stood by me in the most brave and totally committed way afterwards when the attacks came. Jeanne Gerval Arrouf created a beautiful sculpture of the book, bound in barbed wire, locked up with a key, and strung up on a hangman's gibbet, as an homage to its banning.

What are some of the purposes for writing as you see it?

The question of purpose is a difficult one. My drive to write is very clearly, definitely, and unequivocally to tell a story. I love telling stories orally, and I love writing them. I get immense pleasure out of both. The pleasure of making people a gift, and the best gift of all is a narrative. It leaves people free to take what they find in the gift.

So that's my motivation.

But the purpose behind a particular novel is a more cerebral one. The purpose is to deal with subject matter so poignant that only a novel can handle it. In a novel you can put the structure, the central structure, outside the novel and it is still there. In *Getting Rid of It*, for example, the central narrative structure is from before the book starts, and you only find scant references to it so that it remains subliminal for a reader: all three main characters are homeless and jobless because they have lost their jobs that had housing included. Now this is the tragedy of wage slavery. You, a human being, lose everything when your employer, another human being, dismisses you from work.

Now, the unexplored narrative behind these three characters is that they got kicked out by the most innocent of all bosses, just to show the reader that the problem is *structural*, profoundly political, and not a moral issue or a "bad" boss. The bosses in the novel, mainly behind the scenes, were all women so oppressed and helpless that they committed suicide. This was how the three main characters found themselves homeless and hanging in there in precarious jobs at the beginning of the book. What better way could I find to make this point? Or, in the same novel, how when abortion is criminalized, a mere miscarriage makes you a criminal suspect. What are you supposed to do with the fetus?

Can you share a particularly difficult rejection story and how you overcame the emotion of that experience?

I have still not completely overcome the way in which my

2010 novel, *The Malaria Man and Her Neighbours,* was finally rejected. A big publisher in London had taken an option. They read it and liked it but asked for some reworking on lines I thought interesting. I did quite a major rework. They liked it better but asked for a further rework. I wrote it again. Then they refused it. Now what was difficult for me was the three drafts I was left with were very different from each other. They had different numbers of main characters, the point of view changed, and so on. And so then, I ended up liking all three.

They were like three different novels. The feeling of each was different, so I had a lot of difficulty knowing how to complete the process of this novel. I thought at one point of putting all three up on an Internet site and letting them be. Then, finally, I wrote a fourth version, submitted it to my workers' education publishers in Mauritius, who published it. That was a fantastic experience. There is nothing better than being published locally. The feeling is holistic, the pleasure more tangible. The feedback more immediate. The price more appropriate. And of course, the launch was a great party.

To the extent that I have overcome the experience, I have learned that perhaps I wrote the novel just a little *before I was really ready* for that three-week, all-out night-and-day writing phase. So I was therefore too flexible when people asked for reworks and went too deeply into a rewrite instead of a fine tuning. I did this twice, and then again, the final time.

I love this novel, though. So, that is my greatest satisfaction— as well as, of course, having readers now who also love it and tell me so.

Can you share the story of your first publication (book, article, poem, or otherwise) and what that experience was like—any emotions, contemplations, or lessons associated with it?

When I was six, I was very upset about the death of a second dog. Rover had to be put down because he came from the bush with us, and my parents realized he couldn't get used to the village when we moved to Cala. He would fight with neighbors' dogs and kill them, and then he killed Mr. Nel's cat. I have no recollection who Mr. Nel was, but I still remember that Rover killed Mr. Nel's cat, and as a result he had to be put down. This was difficult, but I got over it when we got another little dog who I called Bonzo. When my parents were away from home on a rare occasion, on the death of my father's father, my brother and I were staying with the woman who cared for me. Bonzo fell ill, and when I couldn't find him, she told me he was playing at the bottom of the garden. And from this, I knew that he was dead. All this death in one go.

So, anyway, unbeknownst to anyone, I wrote an article about my sadness at the death of the two dogs, sent it to a newspaper in some nearby big town, and it was published. My father saw it and showed it to me. My enjoyment at my first publication was totally ruined by the title they gave the piece: "He loved two dogs, but they died." First, they assumed I was a little boy, which I did not appreciate at all. And second, they missed the point of the story which was about grief, not about death. So, I've had problems with titles since a very young age.

At primary school, I wrote and produced two books that have survived. One is called *My Encyclopoedia*, no less, and is a compendium of bizarre facts, collected in alphabetical order and illustrated, too. I actually got to Z. So I've been quite determined to get to the end of things from when I was very young. I still find this quite remarkable. That anyone, least of all myself, can finish *a whole novel*. It is such a big thing, like a symphony. How on earth do I keep it in my head while I'm working on it? I always think I'll never be able to do it again!

At secondary school, I kept a diary for three years every day when I was at boarding school. When our dormitories were burnt down completely in a big fire, one or two of us disobeyed the strictest of instructions and later crept upstairs into the burnt-out shell of a building. I found the diary, all burnt around the edges, and for years kept it in a plastic bag. It followed my parents around for many years as they continued their peripatetic lives and eventually got thrown out by mistake in Umhlanga Rocks.

In 2010, when I was at the Jozi Bookfair for the South African launch of my novel, *The Malaria Man and Her Neighbours*, I bumped into the writer and critic Stephen Grey, who told me he believed he was the first one to publish a poem of mine. I was thrilled to hear this, especially since I have only the vaguest recollection of writing this poem and an even vaguer recollection of having it published. This makes me conclude that I must, for some reason, have been ashamed of it.

What words of advice would you share with a young writer who seeks to craft fiction that makes a difference in the world?

The most important thing, for beginnings, is to take little notes. Jot down rough little notes. Keep them secret so that you cherish them, reject them later, and know they are there. Don't try to make them anything special, just any old thing. Write down things you're sure you'll never use. They are only notes, you must say to yourself. When doing this kind of writing, you might find it leads to what you can create a novel out of.

Read your writing aloud after you've written a burst, just to make sure it sounds like you and not like someone else. This is called *finding your voice*. Everyone has one, but people have been made to feel theirs is not a good one or that it's not good enough of one. It is.

When doing a novel, once you start the big drafting sessions, try to get into contact with the part of you that invents dreams. It is there. It takes a kind of concentration to get in contact with it, but you can. Narrative is natural. Creating it is natural. You can even do it when you're fast asleep. So, to write a novel is no more than disciplining this capacity. No more than guiding it.

Closing Reflections

C hoosing to be a writer is a paradox because you can't really choose—the writing chooses you instead. The stories and poems that beckon your brain and heart are relentless in their prodding—unwilling to remain silent until you flip the switch on your computer or uncap your fountain pen and begin scribbling.

Something.

Anything.

The late short story writer Andre Dubus once wrote that the stories we need to tell are like ghosts that haunt us—hanging around until we finally give them the voices they long to embody. Rainer Maria Rilke, in his profoundly moving *Letters to a Young Poet*, claimed that the poems we need to write demand their own attention, their own space. They refuse to be forced into avenues of pleasing people, earning money, or in any way living like chameleons.

So it is with you. With me. With all of us who pull back our chairs each day and sit down at our desks to write.

We do so day after day for a lot of reasons. But if we make a lifelong pursuit of doing it, then the only motivation that works forever is faith. We write because we believe.

Writers often get prodded into a certain genre of existentialism, of detached questioning of everything and assumptions that we don't believe, we doubt. In fact, the very opposite is the truth.

Both parts of this humble volume illustrate the undeniable fact that we write not because we're clueless or because we have no faith. Instead, we write because we believe—because we have a need to believe and because words provide that bridge that allows us to wake up every day and hold a light to the heart of the story.

We believe in the reality of pain.

We believe in the beauty of redemption.

We believe in the necessity of hearing stories—whether true or false.

We believe in the joy of creating stories.

We believe that we are not alone.

We believe that at the end of the day—no matter how tightly our society has wrung its words out in the arenas of politics, media, criticism, fear, hate, or scandal—words still matter. Words still move the world.

We believe.

And even though all logic would suggest otherwise—would point to the pointlessness of creating, the sheer enormity of the task, the cost-effectiveness models of what we do—we do it anyway. We keep going. That's either the definition of lunacy or the definition of faith.

In Fyodor Dostoevsky's heart-wrenching novel *Crime and Punishment*, we meet Raskolnikov, a young man who has said to God, to the universe, to himself, that life is meaningless. That nothing matters. That our actions have no bearing on the weight of the world and the condition of our souls. He theorizes that he can kill his old landlady and feel no shame, no mourning, no piercing of his own soul.

And for hundreds of pages we follow Raskolnikov's soul as it travels this path of *trying* not to have faith—of trying *not* to believe. But against the force of grace at work in the world, he cannot withstand. Eventually, he sinks to his knees and realizes that actions matter. Life matters. Words matter. It all matters.

None of us can resist the relentless force of faith unleashed along every corridor of the lives we walk. No matter how hard we try to ignore the stories that show us themselves, calling us to give them voice, we can't ever win. In essence, then, the life of a writer is the glorious life of a loser, of one who has heard the stories calling in the wilderness and who has given up any notions of pride through unbelief. Instead, the writer throws up his or her hands and says, *Fine. You win. I'll keep going. I'll write the stories and the poems and the essays and the songs and the memoirs and the novels you send my way. I can no longer resist. I lose.*

And in so losing the safety of unbelief, we find a life full of victories. Small victories, to be sure, but victories nonetheless. As Andre Gide once wrote, "In order to discover new lands, we must be willing to lose sight of the shore for a very long time."

As writers, we leave behind the shores of pretension and embrace the new lands that beckon us onward. We write by faith, not by sight.

We write because we believe, and we write every day to help ourselves continue to believe. Whatever happens in your journey as a writer from here onward, may you hold onto the vision of new lands that shimmer on your horizon. Be willing to hear the stories that beckon you. Be willing to give them voice. And in so doing, know your own.

About the Author

Luke Reynolds has taught seventh through twelfth grade English in public schools in Connecticut and Massachusetts, as well as Composition at Northern Arizona University. He is the co-editor of *Burned In: Fueling the Fire to Teach* (Teachers College Press, 2011) and of *Dedicated to the People of Darfur: Writings on Fear, Risk, and Hope* (Rutgers University Press, 2009). His book, *A Call to Creativity: Writing, Reading, and Growing with Students in an Age of Standardization* (Teachers College Press, 2012) looks at the prospect and purpose of education in a new way. Additionally, he is the author of *A New Man: Reclaiming Authentic Masculinity from a Culture of Pornography* (Stonegarden Publishing, 2007) and his writing has appeared in *Tucson Weekly, The Arizona Daily Sun, The Sonora Review, Hunger Mountain, The Hartford Courant, Mutuality, The Believer,* and *The Writer.* He holds an MA in Creative Writing from Northern Arizona University and has done graduate work at Boston College's Lynch School of Education. His writing for young adults and children is represented by Ammi-Joan Paquette of the Erin Murphy Literary Agency.

Lightning Source UK Ltd.
Milton Keynes UK
UKOW040631290113

205531UK00003B/121/P